Cultivating the Buddhist Heart

Cultivating the Buddhist Heart

How to Find Peace and Fulfillment in a Changing World

Nichiko Niwano

translated by
Susan Murata *and* Suzanne Trumbull

Kosei Publishing Co. · Tokyo

This book was originally published in Japanese by Kosei Publishing Co. under the title *Shinden o tagayasu*.

A Note on Names
Names of premodern Japanese—people living before the Meiji Restoration of 1868—follow the Japanese form, family name before personal name. Names of Japanese living after the Restoration are given in Western style, personal name before family name. Chinese names are rendered according to the Wade-Giles system.

Cover design by Abinitio Design, Japan. The text of this book is set in a computer version of Palatino.

First English edition, 2008

Published by Kosei Publishing Co., 2-7-1 Wada, Suginami-ku, Tokyo 166-8535, Japan. Copyright © 2008 by Kosei Publishing Co.; all rights reserved.

ISBN 978-4-333-02322-6

CONTENTS

PREFACE

I often picture the Buddha in my mind's eye, something that is a matter of course for a Buddhist. We know quite a bit about Shakyamuni, the historical Buddha. His teachings were compiled in numerous sutras, and his Dharma, or Law, has been handed down through the ages from teacher to disciple. Much has been written about the Buddha's preaching travels and about his personality. These writings are a rich source of important information and are well worth studying. All the same, I enjoy thinking about what Shakyamuni must have looked like some twenty-five hundred years ago, what he might have thought and done in certain situations, and what might have concerned him the most.

Of all the images of the Buddha that pass through my mind, the one I find most appealing is that of the missionary Shakyamuni, walking hither and yon to preach the Truth and the Dharma. He traveled across a vast and humid land, sometimes preaching to kings, sometimes to great crowds. At other times, he spoke of the Truth and the Dharma to individuals whom he encountered on his travels. Shakyamuni must have been so full of compassion, so eager to share his discovery of the Truth and the Dharma, that he felt compelled to speak to as many people as he could. His travels ended only when he entered nirvana.

We are able to come into contact with the Truth and the Dharma today precisely because Shakyamuni attained enlightenment and because he preached far and wide on what he attained from this enlightenment. One day, when I was speaking about the Buddha's missionary travels, I was asked, "How exactly do you envision Shakyamuni in his role as a missionary?" I answered with relish, thinking all the while of the myriad facets of the Buddha that I had glimpsed in the sutras and in the writings of such modern Japanese scholars as Hajime Nakamura and Shuichi Maida.

"I see Shakyamuni gazing slightly down and ahead, his eyes on the road just a short distance before him as his feet tread firmly but silently forward, one assured step at a time. He wears a simple patched robe, and a fresh, clean fragrance emanates from him. That is how I envision him."

Even as I replied, in my mind I joined my hands in reverence to the Shakyamuni whom I had portrayed. A silent Shakyamuni, eyes slightly cast down as he gazes at the path immediately ahead—there is much to be learned from this vision. The Buddha looks neither into the distance nor behind, but focuses steadily just a few paces ahead as he moves forward with determination, step by step. He concentrates totally on what lies just ahead, dedicating his whole being to it. His concentration is never disturbed by his surroundings. In my portrayal of him, I believe Shakyamuni is looking within himself, always reflecting on the truth about life and the reality of human nature.

His stance is relaxed, with no sign of tension in his shoulders, as he proceeds calmly and quietly. Here I envision the Buddha's deep compassion, a compassion that compels him to preach the Truth and the Dharma to others. He is convinced that the truth to which he has been enlightened will achieve the salvation of all humankind, and so he preaches the Buddhist Way to the people around him. That is my vision of Shakyamuni.

The Buddha made an "original vow" to lead all people to salvation, and to that end he traveled far and wide to preach. The Buddha's life shows us the Way to true happiness.

"Simplicity" is the theme I set for myself when I succeeded my father, Nikkyo Niwano, as the president of Rissho Kosei-kai in 1991. I chose this theme from a deeply held aspiration to understand the essence of things and to live by those truths. What is Buddhism's primary teaching? What is the essence of faith? What are Rissho Kosei-kai's goals? What is most important to human beings? These are the questions I set out to answer.

As I pursued these questions, it became clear to me that Shakyamuni and the truth that he realized through enlightenment are the starting point of Buddhism. There have been many people over the centuries who have sought to convey the Dharma, but their source is the same: Shakyamuni. It did not take me long to reach this conclusion. More than ever, I found myself envisioning Shakyamuni. It is my prayer that, as a believer in the Buddhist faith, I may meet Shakyamuni in my mind, hear his words, and genuinely succeed to his enlightenment.

The next task I set myself was to learn the exact nature of Shakyamuni's spiritual awakening and what lay at the root of his enlightenment. To put this another way, I sought to see if it was possible to condense Shakyamuni's teachings into a single statement. A clear and succinct presentation of the Buddha's teachings, I felt, was the best way to reach as many people as possible in the contemporary era, and to show how, here and now, they can be truly reborn as human beings.

My quest led me to delve into the writings of the great teachers of the past and to reflect on their words. The conclusion I reached from my study was the law of transience, that all things are impermanent and undergoing constant change. This is the first principle of Buddhism, the very root and essence of Shakyamuni's enlightenment. That was a thrilling moment, for I found myself instantly freed of all worries and concerns, as if a bright ray of sunshine had cleared away the fog in which I had been enveloped until that moment.

Having reached this conclusion about the essence of Shakyamuni's enlightenment, I now understood what is essential for us to live fully as human beings. Buddhism's primary teaching of transience shows us how we can be reborn even as we live in the here and now. Ever since becoming aware of this essential truth, I have dedicated myself to conveying the Truth and the Dharma to others.

Life is precious and irreplaceable, never to be experienced a second time. Yet how many of us really treasure each moment of every day as we should? Shakyamuni did not teach us how to satisfy our human desires. What he did do was enable us to appreciate, through recognition of the Truth and the Dharma, how precious is this life that we have been given, and how grateful we should be for the gift.

I believe Shakyamuni had only one objective on his missionary travels, and that was to convey the Truth and the Dharma to people and thereby enable them to recognize the true path to salvation. What the Buddha sought was a great transformation, and he did this by tilling the field of the heart of everyone he met.

The year 1998, when the Japanese version of this book was published, was the sixtieth anniversary of the founding of Rissho Kosei-kai. On that occasion I proclaimed "each and every one of us tilling the field of the heart" as the organization's objective. This sprang from my wish for Rissho Kosei-kai to be a true Buddhist organization. I titled the book *Shinden o tagayasu* (Tilling the Field of the Heart) to express the aspiration to emulate Shakyamuni and to realize his original vow.

In the pages that follow I have distilled topics I have discussed in my travels around Japan. I realize that the text is simple and even somewhat repetitive. All I can say in my defense is that the repetitiveness indicates points that I particularly wished to stress. In addition, phrases like "the Truth and the Dharma" and "the first principle of Buddhism" mean more or less the same thing—the law of transience. Likewise, phrases like "the Buddha's teachings" and "Buddhism" refer to all the teachings of the Buddha—the so-called eighty-four thousand gates to the Dharma. Finally, I have drawn inspiration from and quoted many people, including teachers of earlier times. I owe them a great debt of gratitude and give thanks to all of them.

I wrote this book in the wish to clarify what it means to emulate Shakyamuni, the founder of Buddhism, and the essence of what he wished to convey to us, and to share the fact that we find true happiness and a sense of what makes life worth living through following the Truth and the Dharma. I hope that the book will be read in this spirit. If readers find it helpful, I will be happy.

CHAPTER 1
LIVING IN TRANSIENCE

Transience, the Essence of Shakyamuni's Enlightenment

The law of transience—this is the essence of Shakyamuni's enlightenment, and the one thing he wants us to know.

Everyone would like to be happy. We all want to live fulfilling lives. Some will find happiness in obtaining something they have always wanted; others value most a sound family; still others live for their work or a hobby. These are all fragile elements that may disintegrate at any moment, however. It is difficult to attain true happiness through such things.

What then is true happiness? What is it that gives real purpose to our lives? Shakyamuni answered these questions by showing us the Way. Often referred to as "the eighty-four thousand gates to the Dharma," Shakyamuni's teachings are indeed numerous. But all of them offer solutions to life's many problems and quandaries, and all teach the Way to true happiness.

If we had to learn all Shakyamuni's teachings before we could understand the message he conveys, most of us would never succeed. Fortunately, a short-cut to understanding the teachings exists, and that is to clarify what lies at their source, the essence that re-veals the Way to true happiness, the fundamental principle that makes life worth living.

What is this essence? What is the most important part of Shakyamuni's teachings? What is that one thing he wanted us to know? The answer can be found in the doctrines "All things are impermanent" and "All things are devoid of self," which are two of the Three Seals of the Law. "All things are impermanent" is the teaching that everything in this world is constantly changing, never remaining the same even for an in-stant. "All things are devoid of self" teaches that nothing in this world exists in isolation; everything is interrelated and interdependent. The last of the Three Seals of the Law is known as "Nirvana is eternally tranquil" and refers to a realm where all sufferings are extinct, a truly free and secure place, the absolute state of serenity.

If we pursue this line of thinking even further, we can condense the two central doctrines until finally they are represented by a single word: *transience*. This concept, once it is firmly recognized, enables us to find the fundamental solution to all the kinds of suf-fering that we may encounter, without losing sight of ourselves or falling into despair. When life is going smoothly, this teaching keeps us humble and thank-ful. That truth, that Law, is the law of transience, the core of the Buddha's teachings. Some people say Bud-dhism is hard to believe and understand and is forbidding and off-putting. But if it is condensed into the law of transience, the essence of Shakyamuni's enlightenment, it is very easy to understand and approach.

Everything is constantly changing

Transience means that nothing ever stays the same but undergoes constant change. It is change of position, change of circumstance, change of form, change of consciousness: change in all respects, change that is never ceasing.

The life of a plant is transient. The planted seed sprouts, its stem grows, leaves emerge, flowers bloom, and the plant bears fruit. For human beings, transience is the birth of a child who grows to attend school, to marry, and to have children. All forms of life are constantly undergoing change in this way. Transience is what life is all about.

Our bodies, hearts, and minds change from one instant to the next. At this very moment the cells in our bodies are growing, dying, and being reborn. Every day our hair and nails grow a little. We gain or lose weight. We learn new things and forget old ones. No one is the same from one day to the next.

Our hearts and minds can undergo even more vigorous change. The unhappy person who once complained every day can change so dramatically that each day becomes a day of thanksgiving. The self-centered person can suddenly awaken to the joy of serving others. The unresponsive person can learn to react and speak up, always with a smile.

That all things are constantly changing is the common thread that binds everything in the universe. Change is normal, change is to be expected, and this means there is always a way to free ourselves from suffering.

A universe of flux and creation

Weather is a constantly changing phenomenon, of course. The skies are clear one moment, cloudy the next, this is followed by rain, and so on. Even dirt, a seemingly inert substance, is teeming with microscopic life that changes from one moment to the next. Great boulders and small stones alike are gradually worn down, and even iron and steel eventually rust away. Likewise, the stars in the heavens are constantly dying and new ones are being born from one moment to the next.

Our own sun is a bright fiery orb today, but in eons past, we are told, it was much dimmer. When the fierce hydrogen fusion to which the sun owes its brightness eventually dies down, the sun will expand into a sphere reaching to the orbit of Mars, swallowing our planet in the process. Right now the sun gives off just the right amount of light and heat to support the multitude of life forms existing on Earth. The day will come, however, when no life can exist on our planet. This is another manifestation of transience.

Earth, too, is constantly changing. In primeval times most of Japan was at the bottom of the sea, and we know that the archipelago was once connected to the Asian continent. Underground rivers flow deep beneath our feet, and even deeper lies seething magma. Earth as a planet is a single, constantly changing, living entity. Economics, culture, and thought are also changing day by day. Nothing in this world remains unchanged. The only eternal truth is the law of transience, a truth that will never change even billions of years hence.

The eternal and universal law

Shakyamuni was seeking the fundamental deliverance from all the sufferings of human existence when he entered into meditation under the Bodhi tree. He attained enlightenment at daybreak on the morning of December 8.

There are many opinions as to exactly what was the truth discovered by Shakyamuni. Some say the nature of his enlightenment is not clear; others maintain that he discovered the law of dependent origination; still others insist that what he discovered was the reality of all existence; and so on. From all that I have learned, my conclusion is that Shakyamuni discovered the law of transience.

That everything in the world is constantly changing, never staying the same from one moment to the next, is the essence of transience. That, I believe, is the conclusion Shakyamuni reached in his enlightenment. But, you may say, that is such an obvious and simple concept. Why, anyone could think of it. Surely the truth discovered by such an extraordinary person as Shakyamuni must be complex, profound, and refined.

Yet the conclusion Shakyamuni reached was a most simple and mundane truth. I find it extremely gratifying that the great and wise Shakyamuni in his enlightenment should have discovered that most universal and simplest of laws, the transience of all things, and in his all-encompassing compassion took it upon himself to show this clearly to us. The law of transience was true before Shakyamuni's enlightenment, is still true in the present, and will be true in the future. It permeates our world and the entire universe. Transience therefore is both eternal and universal.

Whether we realize it or not, the law of transience applies to one and all, no matter what one's faith may be. It is the great law of the cosmos, applying to all living things. Not only is Buddhism easy to understand when it is compressed into the law of transience; it also becomes much more real and personal. The act of recognizing that law and living in this recognition is the Way of Buddhism.

Change and Creation

The law of transience far surpasses human understanding, light and dark, good and evil. It is boundless.

The opening passage of the *Heike monogatari* (Tale of the Heike), Japan's classic early-thirteenth-century epic of the Taira clan, refers to the Buddhist concept of transience in this famous passage:

> The moaning of the bell of Jetavana Vihara
> Echoes in the transience of all things.
> The color of the *shala* flowers
> Conveys the law that whatever prospers
>   always must wither.

Unfortunately, this passage emphasizes the sadness and pathos of the fleeting world and by its very fame has severely limited the typical Japanese interpretation of the concept of transience.

Transience can be considered a cause for grief and sorrow because it encompasses aging and death, the fall of nations, and the demise of cultures. That is only one aspect of transience, however. It also encompasses joy and pleasure, happiness and all that makes life worth living, the formation and development of things, and creation. For example, the birth and growth of a child are a matter of joy, pleasure, and encouragement to parents and other family members. This is only one example of the formative, developmental, and creative aspects of transience. Thus, there are two facets to transience, and it is important to recognize both. We should be especially careful to keep in mind the positive facet, that of formation, development, and creation.

The transience of both suffering and pleasure

I met him about five years ago, a man in his late forties, the owner of a small business with a few employees. He had the misfortune to be saddled with a huge debt as a result of the bankruptcy of a client company and a succession of business failures. He told me how he went from client to client and from bank to bank, begging for their understanding and patience while he did everything he could to repay his debt.

At the time of our meeting, the man still owed a great deal of money. The burden was a heavy one, he told me. "It's such a huge sum, nearly impossible to pay back, but my family and my employees are all doing their best." He continued, "I consider this a test that's demanded of me. That way there's some pleasure to be found in what normally would be suffering. A small company that was once doing well has been forced to change course because of a big debt. I can see now that this really is an ever-changing world. I'm still in debt, but every day is fulfilling."

Far from feeling gloom and despair, the man spoke with a smile that belied the heavy burden under which he labored. I was impressed by his manner and deeply moved that the acknowledgment of transience had enabled him to accept and endure his suffering with such grace.

The world is like a turbulent sea in which we are as likely to be pounded by great waves of suffering and grief as we are to ride on waves of pleasure and joy. The thing to remember is that whatever our present condition, it is not going to last forever and even at this instant is shifting. Once we accept that things inevitably change, it becomes possible not only to persevere but also to persevere with a smile. In suffering and sorrow are found subtle tones and flavors of life that could never be savored otherwise. In the midst of pleasure and happiness, the knowledge that this cannot last forever keeps us from forgetting the truly important things of life. The knowledge that all things are impermanent and changing helps us to see beyond superficial joys and sorrows deep into the essence of life and gives us the wherewithal to lead our lives positively.

This ephemeral world

We do not know what will happen tomorrow. We need to be prepared for anything at any time. We cannot allow ourselves to plunge into despair and become desperate when something unexpected happens. The way to be prepared is to acknowledge the law of transience.

We experience all kinds of difficulties. Some creep up on us, while others hit us suddenly. A parent in a healthy, happy family may suddenly lose his or her job. Someone in the family may have an automobile accident, someone may die, or the family ties may disintegrate. A terrible natural disaster may occur. Such things happen all the time. Misfortune is always difficult to bear. We may suffer so much, our despair and frustration may run so deep, that we lose the will to live. It is to be hoped that we will be relieved of such pain as soon as possible. At the same time, we need to see our suffering through, to drink in the pain and sorrow right down to the last drop. There is meaning, I believe, in shedding tears, in confronting suffering straight on, in pushing ourselves to the limits of sorrow and affliction, because these are the kinds of experiences that enable us to clearly see the transience of all things. This clear vision allows us to see the way toward relief and help in the truest sense.

The bitter taste of pain and sorrow forces us to acknowledge that human beings are frail creatures and some things are beyond our control. This realization is what brings us to acknowledge the law of transience. Surprisingly, it is most often when we are at the lowest point in our lives that we discover the strength to rally.

How often have you wondered, "Why me? Why is it that this misfortune has struck only me?" No one knows why. There is no simple explanation. All we can do is acknowledge that all things are transient, that transience encompasses pain and suffering, and that this is an ephemeral world.

The limits of human endeavor

The ups and downs of life are numerous and varied. There may be more suffering and pain than anything else, but new joys and pleasures are to be found in overcoming grief and anguish. Transience is an unlimited power that transcends limited human abilities. Many things in this world cannot be resolved by human endeavor. Of course we should always make the effort to resolve any problem we encounter. Human endeavor, however, is indeed a small thing when confronted by the infinite capacity to change. It is only natural that we despair.

The instant we acknowledge that we are powerless, our lives can undergo a great transformation. We are humbled; just as when a person of great wealth has experienced the pain of losing all those riches, we discover something that is much more important. We are suddenly able to see clearly that we have been worrying over small things when there is something infinitely greater.

Seeing clearly is not at all the same as giving up. It means discerning the limitations of human ability by having been overwhelmed by unexpected changes and having experienced transience firsthand. We all wish to live happily, but life does not always go the way we want. Everyone encounters suffering at one time or another. That is what transience is all about. It is only when we have the clear vision to see this fundamental fact that our lives truly begin. That recognition of the obvious allows us to find the strength to forge our future.

Transience and Dependent Origination

The individual exists here and now, in a net of interdependence with everything in the universe. All things exist in a relationship of mutual support.

Everything is always changing. To be more specific, things change according to the law of dependent origination. The Udana (Solemn Utterances of the Buddha) defines dependent origination this way: "When this exists, that exists; when this arises, that arises. When this does not exist, that does not exist; when this ceases, that ceases."

A similar definition is given by Shariputra, one of Shakyamuni's ten great disciples, in the Samyutta-nikaya (Collection of Grouped Discourses). Shariputra uses the analogy of a bundle of reeds to describe the doctrine of dependent origination. It is difficult to make a single bundle of reeds stand upright, but if two bundles are leaned against each other, both will stand. Everything in the world supports something else.

Let us suppose two people get into a fight. One person does something that angers the other. This is the principle of "When this exists, that exists" or "When this arises, that arises." Of course, this is a very narrow interpretation of the doctrine of dependent origination.

"When this exists, that exists" means that all things are related. This applies not only to human relationships; it encompasses the entire world like a great net. Everything is constantly changing within the context of this net. All things are related and interact and support one another. That is the doctrine of dependent origination. The rain falls, the wind blows, the flowers bloom, and the leaves fall, all in a network of interaction and interdependence.

Another principle often discussed in the same connection is that of causes and conditions. Everything that occurs does so as a result of certain causes and conditions. A single cause alone is insufficient; only with the introduction of a set of conditions does something result. The interaction of causes and conditions has a universal dimension, encompassing both space and time. Because its expanse is infinite, it is virtually impossible to pinpoint the exact causes and conditions of each incident that occurs. The emotions of joy or anger triggered within us cannot easily be explained by, or traced to, any single cause or condition. It is impossible for our limited human reason to grasp the infinite chain of relationships behind everything that takes place.

Relationships

We interact every day with a wide variety of people: family members, neighbors, fellow workers, and others. When things go well, we are happy and each day is enjoyable, but when relationships start to fall apart and friction occurs, we suffer. The best way to cope with this is to realize and accept the law of transience, the fact that everything undergoes constant change.

When a relationship with another person seems to be breaking down, we tend to believe that the tension and unhappiness will last forever. We become bitter and complain, and feel caught in an unending circle of accusation and despair. No situation continues forever, though. Whether things are good or bad, they always change. Much is due to causes and conditions over which we have no control. Still, to a certain degree it is possible to initiate change. One way is to stop criticizing the other person, and instead look within oneself to acknowledge one's own deficiencies. This will encourage the other person to do likewise, and then at last both can work together to heal the rift.

I am sure many people have resolved conflicts in this way. Those who are able to acknowledge their own failings are also able to go one step further and express sincere gratitude that their adversary provided them with the opportunity to look into their own hearts. This is a significant step, which is made possible through recognition of the laws of transience and dependent origination. This recognition will usually change things dramatically.

Consider your relationships within the context of the Dharma. Then you will see that all your encounters, especially those that are difficult, are marvelous opportunities to acknowledge and accept your own failings. This is something well worth giving thanks for, because it opens the way to changing yourself. We all change according to conditions, and we also serve as conditions to encourage change around us. Changing yourself is the best way to change an unhappy situation into a happy one.

Remember, do not change yourself simply because

you want the other person to acknowledge his or her own failings in the same way. The real reason we should endeavor to correct our failings is our own spiritual advancement, for that is what will put us in harmony with our surroundings.

By acknowledging that all things are constantly changing, and by perceiving ourselves within this context of constant change, we are able to see that we exist through our relationships with others. It is realization of this essential principle that will eliminate conflict and bring true harmony to the world.

We are all related
Put simply, dependent origination is the doctrine that we are all related. In chapter 3 of the Lotus Sutra, "A Parable," we read this passage:

> Now this triple world
> All is my domain;
> The living beings in it
> All are my children.

These are the words of the Buddha. If we are all children of the Buddha, it means we are all related, we are all brothers and sisters.

In his book *The Buddha in the Robot,* Masahiro Mori, professor emeritus of the Tokyo Institute of Technology, says we are related to everything in the universe. Life is not limited to organic matter, he points out, but is shared by inorganic matter as well. There is life in hydrogen and sodium, too, he says. Not only people, animals, and plants but minerals as well have life.

Mori goes on to note that our human ancestry extends well beyond our parents, grandparents, and great-grandparents. Our lineage, he writes, goes back much further, to the primates from which we are descended, to amoebas, atoms, and elementary particles. By extension, everything in the universe is related to everything else.

The more we learn about the doctrine of dependent origination, the stranger and more wonderful does our own existence in the here and now become. We live in the present because of causes and conditions unbounded by either time or space. We could not have been born into this world without our parents, and they in turn derive their lives from our common ancestors. Looking deeper, we see how we are supported in our existence by many people and things in a complex web of infinite relationships.

Air, sunlight, water, earth, all contribute to our existence. There can be no denying that everything in the universe is related to everything else; all are brothers and sisters within the infinite. The universe, and the planet Earth within it, all make up one great life. Each of us is born and leads his or her individual life within this one great life. Once life is perceived in this greater context, it becomes easy to acknowledge our relationship with all other animals, plants, and indeed everything in the universe.

Recognizing the Truth and the Dharma

Whether we express it as a sudden feeling, knowing, awareness, or enlightenment, what is important is to recognize the Truth and the Dharma.

The truth that Shakyamuni discovered is the core of Buddhism. For the Buddhist believer, the most basic act is to recognize and acknowledge that truth revealed by Shakyamuni's enlightenment and conveyed by the Dharma. Buddhism is not a faith that requires us to consult the divine for our every action.

To recognize the truth is to attain enlightenment. You may have assumed that enlightenment is the province of the buddhas, that it is not something a mere mortal can attain. I purposely used the word *recognize* because I thought it would make attaining enlightenment seem more approachable than lofty terms. I could have said "know" or "become aware of," but the meaning would be the same.

The Truth and the Dharma ultimately are the same. From his enlightenment Shakyamuni discovered the truth, and the Dharma is how he conveyed it to others. To live by the Truth and the Dharma is the essence of Buddhism. To recognize the Truth and the Dharma is to know with one's innermost being, without conscious reasoning, that all things in the world are undergoing constant change. It is to recognize and to live by the law of transience.

I first intuitively understood transience when my mother died. I think this is true for many people. Most often it is through the death of a loved one or at a moment of similar significance that we are really able to grasp what transience means. This instantaneous recognition is extremely important, for even though it occurs as a momentary flash, it happens deep within our being and is equivalent to enlightenment.

Picture a blank piece of paper in your mind. Now imagine that a burning spark drops on the edge of the paper and sets it alight. Our sudden awareness of the meaning of transience is like the tiny flame that spreads to burn up the sheet of paper. In the same way our sudden recognition of transience spreads rapidly through our entire being. In a flash of recognition we can become aware of the Truth and the Dharma.

To know and to act

I remember being taught that to learn, to know, is the most basic of human activities. Knowledge is an essential factor in every human undertaking. In the world of religion, the tendency is to emphasize action—such as ascetic practices for spiritual advancement—over knowledge. But knowledge is at the root of all action or practice. It is only through a knowledge of Buddhism that practice becomes possible. If we did not know the Buddha's teachings, we could not possibly practice them. To know is not just to amass knowledge; it is to know with one's whole being, to sense the truth with one's very life.

"Knowing is easy, doing is difficult," goes a common saying. But I believe the opposite: "Knowing is difficult, doing is easy." Action or practice comes naturally when we know what is important. We cannot concentrate when we do not know what is really important, and our days are aimless as a result.

The important thing to know is the law of transience that lies at the heart of the Buddha's teachings. Well, you may ask, how does one go about knowing or recognizing transience? What does one have to do to acquire this knowledge? I do not believe any special practices are required. The knowledge can be achieved by intuition. Transience is something that is felt and recognized in the briefest of moments. No special austerities or practices are required. The act of knowing is in and of itself the most important practice.

Transience means only that all things are in a state of constant change. This is simple enough for anyone to understand. All we need to do is see and accept the events in our daily lives just as they occur. Likewise, human relationships and social issues are always changing. If you take a close look, you can see for yourself what transience is. Simply watching nature take its course is another way of understanding it. We need only to watch, carefully and quietly, the changes that take place before our eyes.

Looking deep within oneself, as Shakyamuni did when he meditated under the Bodhi tree, is an excellent way to come to understand transience. Other ways are also possible. In Rissho Kosei-kai, these include such practices as dissemination and *hoza* (Dharma circle) sessions, and our daily devotions before the home altar. Each of these gives us the strength and where-withal to teach the Dharma to others. At the same time, they are useful in helping us to concentrate on the Truth and the Dharma, in helping us to sense and know transience.

Still, I would like to stress that while the kinds of practices I have described can be useful, what is most important is to know and recognize the Truth and the Dharma. Doing so fills us with joy, a joy we long to share, a joy that compels us to disseminate the Bud-dha's teachings and guide others to the Way. There is much happiness to be achieved in transmitting the Dharma to others. To do so deepens our own understanding. Recognition of the Truth and the Dharma and dissemination go hand in hand.

The Buddhist faith teaches us that all suffering can be resolved by knowing and recognizing the Truth and the Dharma that Shakyamuni discovered through his enlightenment.

Human Beings Are Destined to Die

The only way to overcome death, the greatest suffering that afflicts human beings, is to recognize the law of transience. Gazing unflinchingly at death, let us give thanks for the life we have here and now.

"I was once as you are. Soon you will be as I am." Those words are inscribed at the entrance to an Italian cemetery. The message is to the living from the dead, and it means that sooner or later we all go to the grave.

Religion teaches us to be grateful for the life we are given, and that at the end of each life is death. From the moment that we are born until the day we die, our life is one of transience. When we think back on people's lives, we usually think only of how they conducted their lives, but it is death that completes a life. Buddhism conceives of life and death as a single concept. If there is no death, there can be no life: Each is part of the other.

Some people cringe on even hearing the word *death*. But we should be grateful for life precisely because it is followed by death. Life is fulfilled by our unflinching acceptance of its natural end. No one in human

history has ever been immortal. Even Shakyamuni
lived only for eighty years. All life is finite. The law of
transience emphasizes this fact to us.

According to the Sutra of the Great Decease, just
before Shakyamuni's death he uttered the following
words to his disciple Ananda: "Do not grieve. Parting
with a loved one is as unavoidable as that the living
eventually must die. Apply yourself faithfully, and you
should be able to separate yourself from all worldly
desire."

The mother who lost her child

One day a young woman whose son had died of illness came crying to Shakyamuni: "Please save my
child. Bring him back to life." Shakyamuni instructed
the young mother to seek out a household in the village where death had never occurred. She went eagerly
from house to house, but was unable to find any home
in which no one had ever died. She was saved by
Shakyamuni's words: "Every person who is born must
one day die."

You may ask how this mother was saved. After all,
she requested Shakyamuni to bring her son back to
life, yet all he did was have her search for a home
where death was unknown. But Shakyamuni surely
felt the mother's grief as if it were his own. No sorrow
is greater than that of a mother who has lost a child.
Shakyamuni not only did not respond to the woman's
plea; he also made no attempt to explain to her why
her child had died. I believe that for Shakyamuni it
was most important to get this mother to comprehend
the law of transience. With his help, she was able to
understand and accept that all that lives must one day

end in death. By recognizing the law of transience, the mother was able to overcome her grief and thus be saved. This is a good example of the meaning of salvation in Buddhism.

When I was young, I never gave any thought to the possibility that my mother might die. But one day she did die. Transience assumes many forms. In my case, it was my mother's death that finally allowed me to comprehend with my innermost being what I had previously only understood intellectually.

Death is unavoidable, and religion teaches us how to cope with the unavoidable. Shakyamuni discovered the law of transience, preached it to one and all, and showed us how we might overcome that greatest of human sufferings. Not a single person has been able to avoid confronting death. Recognize that fact with your heart, and you will be able to accept the inevitability of your own death.

Some people live to be a hundred years old or more, others die in the prime of life, and still others face death when they are yet small children. Each individual has his or her own moment of death. What we all have in common is that someday will surely die. To live is to make one's way toward that inevitable outcome.

There are people who suffer from diseases that cannot be cured with the medical knowledge we have today, and then there are the elderly who face death every day. Some people fight to live even as death draws near. It is not easy to accept one's own death. Confronted by death we are filled with a deep melancholy, an agonizing combination of loneliness and fear. But even that can be overcome if we recognize the fact that no one can avoid death, a recognition that enables us to recognize all existence.

Living in the face of death

Transience simply means that every one of us must one day die. We know this, but somehow we always think it does not apply to us. We avoid the thought of our own demise—death is something that happens to other people. As difficult as it may be, even the healthiest among us should keep in mind that inevitable outcome. No one knows what happens to us after we die, but we do know why death exists. It is because nothing in this world stays the same from one moment to the next.

Confronting death does not mean thinking about what happens afterward. It means accepting one's own demise as inescapable. Through this acceptance we come to realize how wonderful it is that we exist here and now. That realization opens the way to achieving fulfillment in life.

The eccentric Japanese Zen master Ikkyu (1394–1481) once drew a picture of two skulls, representing a husband and wife, with the inscription "Let us live together without fighting. Eventually we will both become like these." How foolish of married couples to fight, Ikkyu seems to be saying. Let them at least be friends while both are still alive.

Since the law of transience makes it clear that death cannot be avoided, the issue is what we can do to make our brief existence as pleasant as possible, for others as well as ourselves. Thinking that way makes it obvious that there is no time to be willfully self-centered. What better way to live than to recognize and give thanks for the life we have been given, relishing every moment we have to share with others?

All of us experience brief moments of awareness of the certainty of our own death. Those moments hold great significance for us because it is then that we realize how important it is to live truly worthwhile lives.

Getting Rid of Ingrained Assumptions

We tend to see things in a fixed and relative way: This is mine. That is his. This is beautiful. That is ugly. In truth, it is all a dream, an illusion.

We are attached to many things: our families, good health, work, wealth, honor, and so on. But no matter how fiercely we cling to these things, one day we will be no more. Our attachments melt away when we sense our approaching end and recognize the truth of transience. There is no point bewailing the loss of all to which we are attached when we know that our life will end. The law of transience compels us to see that everything we thought we had is merely illusion.

The Diamond Wisdom Sutra quotes Shakyamuni thus: "All that appears before us is as a dream, an illusion, a bubble, or a shadow. All is like the dew or lightning. It should thus be contemplated that nothing has reality." Everything is a result of dependent origination, he tells us, and nothing has substance.

Prince Shotoku (574–622), the great Japanese statesman of ancient times who was a devout believer in Buddhism, thought that everything we hold dear— our physical body, daily life, and activities—is but a temporary manifestation. Nothing is certain; only the world of the Buddha is the eternal truth.

The Buddhist term *shunyata,* usually translated as "emptiness," represents this transience, the fact that all things grow, develop, and disappear, that nothing is constant. The Suttanipata (Collection of Sutras), one of the oldest Buddhist scriptures, says, "See that the world is but emptiness, and even death can be overcome." To overcome death is to overcome the sufferings of human existence: birth, aging, illness, and death. Any type of human suffering can be resolved once we accept the law of transience and recognize that all is emptiness.

Realize that everything is constantly changing, and your attachments will greatly diminish in importance. When everything is constantly changing, how foolish warfare is. Recognize that all things in this world are only temporary phenomena, and your attachment to them will lose its hold. The world is empty, without substance. There is nothing in it that belongs to us. If we escape from our attachments, we will escape from all suffering. That is the law of transience.

The Sutra of Cow Dung

One day Shakyamuni stopped people along the road to ask, "Are my fingernails clean or dirty?"

"The Buddha's fingernails are like pearls, the ultimate in cleanliness," was the reply.

Shakyamuni stooped and dug his fingers into a pile of cow dung. "Are my fingernails clean or dirty?" he asked again.

"The Buddha's fingernails are now encrusted with

cow dung and are extremely dirty," was the reply.

Said Shakyamuni, "So you see, everything is constantly changing in the same manner."

This is a simple story, but it has a profound meaning. In using cow dung to illustrate the concept of transience, Shakyamuni questions our assumption that the Buddha's fingernails are clean and cow dung is dirty. He repudiates the very idea of such relative conditions as clean and dirty. We tend to think in terms of relative values—clean and dirty, able and disabled, rich and poor, cheerful and gloomy—but in this sutra the Buddha teaches us that such comparisons are fleeting at best. In a transient world it is meaningless to cling to such comparisons.

The Lotus Sutra is named after a beautiful flower that blooms in muddy water. The magnificent lotus draws its nourishment from the mud. In other words, the mud is vital for the flower to bloom. Thus the lotus flower and the mud are closely tied in a strange and wonderful web of dependent origination. We call the flower beautiful and the mud dirty, but these are arbitrary judgments, as Shakyamuni so cleverly teaches us in the Sutra of Cow Dung.

All Is New

Every day brings new encounters, first meetings. Every day we are reborn.

Transience means that every moment is new, never to be repeated. In the same way, our minds and bodies

are constantly changing. Today is different from yesterday. Each day we live a unique new life. We live
each day assuming that we will continue to exist the
following day. But none of us know if we will live or
die tomorrow.

The law of transience shows us the wonder of our
existence in the present and emphasizes to us how
grateful we should be for each day. "To be given such
a precious life! What a waste it would be to stay idle
today." We should treasure each encounter, humble
ourselves to learn from others, and strive to do our
best, wherever we are, at every moment. That is what
comes to mind when we fully realize how wonderful
it is to be alive.

Every moment is new, and every day is the first
day of your life, never to be repeated. Today is the first
day since the dawning of the universe—no day can be
as wonderful as today. You are reborn every day, so
greet the morning as if you had just been born. Treat
every encounter as if it were the first and could be the
last. Live each moment as if you were newly born,
and life will be fulfilling.

Cherish the moment
In a transient world, the present moment must be cherished. But no matter how hard you try to get all you
can out of the moment, time may speed by quickly,
leaving you behind. Stop to consider that each day is
a unit of life. Live each day to the fullest, and you will
live your whole life to the fullest. Think in terms of
one day instead of an entire lifetime.

As the days accumulate the years pass, seventy for
some, eighty for others. Each day is a mirror reflecting

a whole life span. Most people get up in the morning with a plan. How well they put that plan into effect will tell how they are likely to pass their entire life. If a day represents a whole life, then the morning is the time of birth and the night the time of death. Live each day as if it were the best of your life, and each year, indeed your entire lifetime, will be equally rewarding. If you can look back and say, "I was allowed to experience a most wonderful life," your time alive will have had great value.

It is imperative that we recognize the preciousness of each day, that we apply ourselves wholeheartedly to our work and our family and friends, finding joy in every encounter and living only to give joy to others. To achieve this, we must recognize the law of transience as the foundation upon which to build our lives.

Professor Reiho Masunaga of Komazawa University has said that we should wake up in the morning with hope, live diligently through the day, and go to sleep at night with gratitude. For those of the Buddhist faith, I paraphrase his message as follows: "Wake up in the morning with hope and the pledge to live in the Buddhist Way. Apply yourself with diligence to the task of improving your faith during the day, and go to sleep at night with thanksgiving in your heart." This is the least that a Buddhist can do.

The late Dr. M. Aram, one of the leading figures in the World Conference of Religions for Peace, made a similar statement about those of the Hindu faith: "The day of the Hindu starts with meditation, a reconfirmation of faith, and prayer, continues with love and compassion, and ends with thanksgiving." I am happy to note that Buddhists and Hindus hold precious

the same affirmation of faith, diligence, and thanksgiving. Surely, true happiness is to be found in living
each day in this way.

The same day never comes twice

"Too few know truly that this world is never to be
again." So reads a line of poetry by the philosopher
and educator Nobuzo Mori. Life can be lived only once,
yet how many of us take this knowledge to heart and
truly understand how precious life is?

We know that today can never be repeated, yet at
the same time we assume that tomorrow will be much
like today, and so we let the days slip by. We waste
time because we do not fully grasp the implications
behind the truth that each day is unique. Know with
your whole being as well as your intellect that today
can never be repeated, and you will feel compelled
not to waste even a moment.

Perhaps work went well today, you enjoyed a
number of pleasant encounters, and you were moved
by a passage in the book you were reading. That was
today; tomorrow is a whole new day. The fact that you
have had one fulfilling day does not mean that you do
not have to apply yourself the next day. Each day is
self-contained, with new efforts made and new steps
taken. Every day you create yourself anew. There is no
greater joy in life.

I spent around ten years, from the summer of my
first year of elementary school to the summer of my
first year of high school, in Suganuma, Tokamachi,
Niigata Prefecture, the home of my father, Nikkyo
Niwano, the founder of Rissho Kosei-kai. It was cus-
tomary each year for the head of the PTA to give a

brief speech at the local elementary school graduation ceremony, and the speech always began with the same words: "Today will be lost forever." Child that I was, I did not really know what those words meant. But as I grew older and learned more about the law of transience, I began to grasp how profound they actually were. I see now that an effort was being made to convey to us the importance of each and every day, and that the words were instructions in transience.

We all experience good days, when everything goes well and a sense of thanksgiving comes naturally, and bad days, when nothing goes as we think it should and we end the day feeling disgruntled. Neither the good days nor the bad will ever be repeated, though. We cannot relive the past or live out the future. The best we can do is live in the present to the fullest extent possible, using each day without waste.

We can spend our day giving thanks or voicing complaints. Which we choose depends on whether we have the flexibility and generosity of heart to see the whole picture or whether we are preoccupied with the minor details before us.

CHAPTER 2
THE PRECIOUSNESS OF LIFE

The Preciousness of Life

To be born human is a rare thing. There is nothing as strange and marvelous as life. Everything starts with wonder at the preciousness of life.

Springtime, when new greenery sprouts and flowers bloom, is a season to which most people look forward with pleasure. This was especially true for me during the ten years of my childhood I spent in Suganuma, which was buried under snow for nearly half the year. In late March or early April, the snows began to melt to reveal the pale green of young butterbur stalks.

No less welcome than flowers is the spring grass
Peeking through the mountain snows.

This verse by Fujiwara no Ietaka (1158–1237), one of the poets included in the *Shin kokin wakashu* (New Collection from Ancient and Modern Times), is one of my favorites. The fresh green grass revealed by the melting snow is as much a joyful portent of spring as are the cherry blossoms so lauded by the poets. For me, the butterburs of Suganuma were the harbingers of spring.

Like the changing seasons, human life goes through its own cycle of birth, aging, illness, and death. This is in keeping with Shakyamuni's teaching that all things are constantly changing. A passage in the Dhammapada says:

> Difficult it is being born a human.
> Difficult it is being alive now for those for whom death is inevitable.
> Difficult it is to hear the right teaching of the Buddha.
> Difficult it is to encounter the appearance of buddhas in the world.

To be born as a human being is a rare and marvelous thing. The life we have here and now is all the more precious when we know that we are destined to die. Likewise, the opportunity to hear the Buddha's teachings is a rare event. How wonderful it is that the buddhas have descended to this world! The verse succinctly describes what is most precious in this world, that for which we should give thanks above all else. We have been given life as human beings. The first half of the verse reminds us what an extraordinary thing that is. The second half teaches us the importance of paying reverence to the Buddha, who propounded the Dharma for us, and of taking refuge in the Buddha and his teachings.

Stop and think: "Why do I have life here and now?" What a wonderful thing it is. The person who cannot feel grateful for having life cannot give thanks for anything.

The rarity of being born human

Why were we born into this world as human beings? The life of each of us comes from our parents, who in turn received life from their parents, and from their ancestors long ago. We should be grateful for our existence. We also should stop to reflect on the reason for that existence.

We take life for granted but should pause and think about it. We were not born into this world of our own conscious will. Why then were we born as human beings? An extraordinary power is at work here. We were given life by a power far exceeding human volition. Some call this the power of the Buddha; to others it is the power of God. Human beings, in fact all living things, are given life by the divine grace of God and the Buddha. I am a human being here and now. By the grace of the Buddha I am alive. The more I reflect on this wonder, the more amazed and moved I am, the more deeply grateful I feel.

No one can live without the sun. For that matter, we cannot live without the moon and the stars, or mountains and rivers. Our lives depend on plants, insects, and microbes. Everything within the universe is essential to our existence. The sun rises in the east and sets in the west. Rice and vegetables, animals and fish, thrive from this simple repetition, and by association we human beings who partake of the rice, vegetables, animals, and fish are given life by the sun. We might even say that the sun rises each day just to imbue each and every one of us with life. Air also exists to give us life. The rains fall and the winds blow to give each individual life. We are alive because the entire universe is constantly working to give us life. We do not live of our own free choice, but rather are granted life by all the things that we encounter.

The world contains victory and defeat, pleasure and sadness. We can savor these emotions because we were given life as human beings. If we awaken to this realization, we cannot help being filled with joy and thanksgiving.

One unique life in all the universe

Earth is said to be the only planet in the solar system that can support human life. Earth is one of eight planets circling the sun. The one closest to the sun is Mercury. The next is Venus, then Earth, followed by Mars. Earth is the miracle planet, the only one able to support life. Venus is so close to the sun that it is too hot to do so. Mars is farther away, and it does not appear to have any life forms either. Yet Earth, situated between those two planets, does have life. On a cosmic scale, the differences in the distances of these planets from the sun are minuscule, but they are enough to make all the difference.

It is a mystery among mysteries that the teeming life on Earth is linked in a marvelous chain of causes and conditions. Each individual existence likewise is a wonder and a mystery in itself. The human being lives in the womb for nine months. Through this period we evolve through various stages to become a mammal, and finally to become a human being.

The history of evolution spanning the more than

four billion years since the origin of life on Earth is condensed in this wondrous phenomenon that occurs in the mother's womb. Each and every person's life is a recapitulation of evolution. In all the great expanse of the universe, we alone have received this unique gift of life on the miracle planet called Earth. Our drive to live to the fullest is rooted in the realization that our lives are unique and irreplaceable.

To gaze on life

As long as we are alive, the beating of our heart and our breathing never cease, even when we sleep.

Yoshio Toi, recipient of the Pestalozzi Award for excellence in education, wrote a short poem called "Upon Awakening."

> Upon awakening
> I was alive
> Not dead.
> I was alive
> Without making any effort
> To live,
> Asleep as I was.
> Yet when I awoke
> I was alive.
> In the middle of a
> Brand-new morning
> That never was before
> In ages past,
> I was alive.
>
> No, I was allowed to live.

What a joy it is to wake up and know that one is alive. Those in good health often do not appreciate this. I have heard, however, that those who have experienced a major illness awaken each morning grateful to still be alive. The last line of Toi's verse states, "No, I was allowed to live." We do not live of our own free will but are granted life by a power superior to ourselves. That is a great truth.

Even as we sleep, our lungs continue to function and our hearts continue to pump blood. The body never stops the work of living. We fall asleep and we wake up. We are alive—no, we are allowed to live. Life is truly an extraordinary thing, as close observation not only of ourselves and other human beings but also of other animals and of plants clearly shows.

The Japanese have a special fondness for cherry blossoms. As the warm days of spring approach, the cherry trees burst into splendor. Soon thereafter, the blossoms are carried off by the breeze in a shower of petals. New green leaves replace the blossoms, and in the autumn the leaves fall and the cherry trees wait patiently for their next blossoming in the spring. The life process is a marvel to behold.

The cicada spends a long time buried underground. It comes up for only a week of life above ground. Watch an ant carrying food to its nest. How does it know where to go? Who told the ant to bring food? This is another extraordinary life process. There is no end to the wonders of the life that goes on all around us.

Scientists and scholars can certainly take a more analytic view of the mechanisms of nature. What I see as an amateur when I observe the plants and animals around me is the unique workings of life. The wonder and joy I experience from these observations turn into wonder and joy at the miracle of my own life, my own existence.

The Marvel of Reality

The afterworld is marvelous, but the real world is marvelous, too. Most marvelous of all, however, is that we are given life here and now.

The world is full of awe-inspiring wonders, like the pyramids in Egypt and the famous giant pictures on the surface of the earth in Peru known as the Nasca Lines. No fewer are the marvels closer to home. Many things cannot be explained no matter how hard we try, but the greatest mystery of all is life itself.

It is impossible to encompass the infinite reality around us by human reasoning alone. For example, it is impossible to know what will occur tomorrow. No one knows what happens to us after we die. That is one more wonder we cannot explain. Yet even more fascinating than the mystery of death is the mystery of life.

It is common in religious circles to speak of miracles. I think the greatest miracle of all is that we are given life as human beings to exist in the here and now. That kind of miracle cannot be explained in words. As I wrote above, it is by the grace of the Buddha that we receive life and are able to experience the joys and anguish of human existence and the wonders and worries of the world. Without life we could not feel or experience anything. Know that your own existence is a miracle, and you will surely be filled with thanksgiving for the Buddha's grace.

Dependent origination, ever interacting

Each life is closely connected to the events of the world. Nothing is confined to only one person or one existence. The relationship of all things is the support by which we are able to exist. The ever-interacting and unbounded expanse of dependent origination defies comprehension by reason.

All of life is linked. Flora and fauna, insects and human beings, all living things interact and give life to one another as part of one great life force. For example, we are able to breathe because the plants around us produce the oxygen that we need to do so. At the same time, the carbon dioxide that we expel helps the plants to grow. We and the plants thus are interdependent, part of one and the same great life. There is no greater sorrow than to be cut off from the one great life of which we are all part.

The late Mother Teresa was well known for the dedicated care she gave to dying men and women who had been abandoned by everyone else. She reassured these people by telling them, "You were born into this world because you were needed." Her words gave great comfort to those who had long lived without human contact, for she was reminding them that their lives were as precious as anyone else's and that they were not, after all, cut off from human society.

The following verse, by Hakushu Kitahara (1885–1942), is from his poem "Two Rose Compositions":

> On a rose bush
> A rose blooms.
> There is nothing to wonder at.

A rose blooming on a rose bush is not unusual or wonderful in any way. It is perfectly within the natural order of things. Yet is not this natural order of things baffling? When we observe the infinite workings of the universe, the complex interactions to which we owe our own existence as human beings, we cannot help being filled with awe and joy at the wonder of it all.

The rose, the human being, both are marvels of existence, of precious, irreplaceable life. Everything in this world exists in an ever-interacting and unbounded expanse of dependent origination in which everything depends upon everything else. When we awaken to the wonder of this existence, we become able to empathize with the pain of other human beings, to understand and accept the feelings of others. The key to this awakening is the law of transience taught to us by Shakyamuni.

"I Am My Own Lord throughout Heaven and Earth"

Each of us is one of a kind, unique in the world and in the universe. Nothing is more precious than this unique life.

Legend has it that as soon as Shakyamuni was born he took seven steps and announced, "I am my own

Lord throughout heaven and earth." Common sense
tells us that a newborn baby could not possibly do such
a thing. This legend undoubtedly is intended to illustrate Shakyamuni's greatness, to show how deserving
he is of veneration.

I like to think, however, that the newborn Shakyamuni's words, "I am my own Lord throughout heaven
and earth," were his way of saying that the life of each
and every human being is unique and precious. Each
of us is an existence without a duplicate in all the universe. Shakyamuni's claim "I am my own Lord" is a
statement about the buddha-life that is absolute and
peerless. The famous birth words of Shakyamuni are
an affirmation of the intrinsic value of human life and
of every other existence, all of which partake of the
life of the Buddha. Through his birth and enlightenment, Shakyamuni teaches us of the rarity of all things
in the universe. His enlightenment elucidates the fact
that everything in life has meaning, even sorrow and
suffering.

Shakyamuni alone is not the Lord of this world.
Every human being, every thing, is equally the Lord,
equally distinctive and precious. There is only one
you in this world and in the whole universe. That is a
truly remarkable and priceless thing.

We are all different. Some people have round faces,
others have faces that are square. Some people have
short tempers, others are patient. Some people like to
study, others do not. Whatever our individual traits,
each of us is one of a kind. Transience teaches us that
no two things are ever alike. No two human beings
can be exactly the same. In acknowledging the law
of transience, we accept that each of us is an invalu-

able existence that cannot be compared with anyone else.

Shakyamuni taught us that all life is interconnected in a single great life that is always, and infinitely, changing. Each individual is part of this process of constant change. Each of us exists as an exceptional and ever-changing life. Each has his or her own special personality. Yet even though we appear to be independent, individual beings, at the same time we are all part of a larger, greater life.

The world of the absolute

Human beings have often ignored the interconnectedness of life, destroying nature to satisfy their selfish desires. Buddhism teaches that not only human beings but all life, flowers and insects and even the pebbles along the roadside, is rare and to be cherished. Everything that exists is linked to everything else, helping support all life. In a sense, the world that we know is a single great life, and we are only one small part of that life.

The buddha-life is to be found even in grass and trees, in mountains and rivers. We human beings, however, prefer to distinguish ourselves from all other forms of life, believing that we are of more value than anything else. But Shakyamuni teaches that all life has value. His view of the world transcends the concept of relative worth, which attaches greater importance to one thing than another, judging this to be superior to that. What Shakyamuni sees is the world of the absolute. Everything in the world has life, and everything that lives has irreplaceable value and represents the absolute Law.

Everything is made to live through the one Truth, the one Dharma. Once we realize this, such narrow views as "this is inferior" or "that must be excluded" vanish.

The buddha-nature in everything

Human beings are not superior to everything else. A robot can do things that people cannot; this is what gives the robot value. The truly noble person is the one who recognizes that everything has value. Someone who thinks that he or she has greater value than others and who looks down on other people is not a person to be respected.

This is the view expressed by Masahiro Mori in *The Buddha in the Robot.* He confirms the depth of the Buddhist concept that everything possesses the buddha-nature. The buddha-nature is to be found not in human beings alone but in all things. Another way to put this is to say that everything innately possesses the buddha-nature.

Ryoan-ji, a famous Zen temple in Kyoto, attracts visitors from around the world to view its rock garden, one of Japan's cultural masterpieces. To the Buddha's eye, however, a small pebble alongside the road is of equal value to the famous rocks of Ryoan-ji. What the Ryoan-ji garden does is help us to see this truth: that each and every rock and pebble is precious and distinctive.

The Lotus Sutra teaches us that everything has value, everything is to be extolled. You and I, this flower and that tree, this living being and that robot, all are worthy of praise. Each of us has value and special meaning. We should respect and praise one another, just as we should respect and praise all things. Despite our superficial differences, we are given life by one all-encompassing life force. That is the world that is revealed to us when we acknowledge the law of transience.

The true essence
Dogen (1200–1253), the founder of the Soto Zen sect, wrote the following brief verse about the natural features of the four seasons in Japan:

> In spring, flowers;
> In summer, the cuckoo;
> In autumn, the moon;
> In winter, the snow cold and bright,
>   chilly and bracing.

This poem about the changing seasons captures the true essence of things. Our true essence is our buddha-nature, which is the reality of our innermost being. Our perceptions of the seasons are influenced by our likes and dislikes. But it is self-centered to denounce the summer for being too hot or to praise the spring for its lovely blossoms. The world of the Buddha and the grand realm of nature transcend such self-centered values.

Spring is delightful simply because it is spring. Summer is worthwhile because it is summer. The same is true of autumn and winter. The seasons come to us in their true form—our personal likes and dislikes have nothing to do with the essence of the four seasons. In the same way, we cannot judge someone to be of value simply because she is eloquent or another to be of less worth simply because he is not good at sports.

When we look at things and think about what we see, we tend to pass judgment based on what is convenient for us. We decide that what suits us is good and what does not is bad. But such thinking only narrows our view of the world. As ordinary as people may be, that does not mean they have no value. Each of us is precious. There is no need to rely on excessive humility or false pride when we know that life is glorious in and of itself. The buddha-nature exists in each of us. The precious gift of life that we have been granted provides meaning for our existence.

It is truly a revelation to realize the preciousness of all life, including our own. This knowledge gives us the courage to live to the fullest and helps us to see how wonderful life is.

The Eternal Life of the Buddha

If we look with the eyes of wisdom, we see that human life is eternal. We are sustained by eternal life and are living within eternal life.

To understand the meaning of transience is to recognize that everything in this world is always changing, from the furthest past to the furthest future. Nothing remains the same from one moment to the next. In other words, transience is eternity.

Chapter 16 of the Lotus Sutra, "The Revelation of the [Eternal] Life of the Tathagata," says that the Buddha's life is eternal. If the Buddha's life is eternal, that means our own lives are also eternal. Yet our actual life spans are limited, even as they are subject to constant change. For us, yesterday is different from today. Yesterday has gone and tomorrow is yet to come. It is not possible for us to live yesterday or tomorrow. We have no choice but to live today, to live each day afresh. To live from yesterday to today and from today to tomorrow is, in a sense, a process of living in the "eternal today," in the "eternal now" that is not present, past, or future.

Human beings are like waves in the great sea of the "eternal now." We ebb and flow, live and die. Just as no wave in the sea appears more than once, so no human life is exactly the same as another. Each of us leads a life that is unique, that can never be replicated once it is gone. Yet despite the constant appearance and disappearance of the waves, the great sea exists for eternity.

Life can only be experienced once. Our eternal life ebbs and flows like the tide of a great sea. No human being can be born into the same life again. We live in this world only once, but we live—are allowed to live—within the eternal life of the Buddha.

The world is eternal

Human life is finite, but we are endowed with the ability to recognize the law of transience, the Truth and the Dharma. This makes it possible for us to touch eternity, to join our finite lives with infinite existence.

To recognize the law of transience is to know everlasting life. By joining our limited lives to that of eternity, we are able to live forever. Your life, my life, each is interconnected with everything in this world.

We exist in the constantly interacting and unbounded expanse of dependent origination. Not a single life can be detached from this framework. Our lives are made possible by the complex interaction of all life. Life is not limited to the individual, but extends to all the world. And the life of the world continues regardless of the birth and death of the individual. Every human life must end someday, but the world is eternal.

Buddhism teaches us that the self and the other are one and the same absolute. When we recognize that all life is part of one great life, it is only natural that we should seek to live in harmony with one another. Consider the self-centered person who awakens to the fact that his or her life is one with all of life. With that awareness comes the ability to live in a world without conflict, the world of eternal life.

A word on time

Let us look at the eternal present, eternal life, from another perspective. Our perception of time is defined by the calendar. We think in terms of the day, the month, and the year. We see time as a straight, continuous line. But real time is more than just one day following another in sequence; it is, in fact, three-dimensional rather than linear.

The time that is the present encompasses everything in the past. In terms of human life, the present—the here and now—is a condensation of our past and a portent of our future. Everything we do, everything that happens around us, becomes the causes and conditions of our future. Thus the present carries the accumulation of the past while at the same time it is pregnant with the future. Eternity is contained in each passing minute.

The fact that today is designated as a certain day of a certain month of a certain year is one aspect of reality. The fact that today, this very moment, is finite and yet part of eternity is another. We who live in this present that contains both past and future are in essence living in the eternal now. This is especially true when we strive to live each day to the fullest.

Our perception of time is usually grounded in the present. Buddhism describes this as like standing on a riverbank and watching a boat sail down the river. Zuiryu Nakamura, a former president of Rissho University in Tokyo, writes of this in his book *Honto no michi, Hokekyo* (The True Way, the Lotus Sutra): "We call the instant that exists right now 'the present,' the one that comes before it 'the past,' and the one that comes after it 'the future.' But this is like standing on a riverbank and watching a boat sail by. We refer to the expanse of water that the boat travels before it comes to where we are standing as upstream. When the boat reaches the point where we are standing, we consider it to be right in front of us. And when it passes us, we say it has gone downstream."

He continues, "But the reality of existence is that we live in tandem with the passage of time. The present moment will, in the next instant, become the past, and the future next moment will, in an instant, become the present. This suggests that it is a mistake to speak of time in terms of past, present, and future defined by one fixed moment in the passage of time. Time passes, just as life passes. The past was once the present, and the future eventually will become the present. We live from moment to moment. After all, if we are in the boat, it will always be right in front of us, neither upstream nor downstream."

I think this passage illustrates well that we live in the eternal now. We are riding in the boat and floating along the stream of time. Acknowledging this gives us the strength and the motivation to lead our lives in the now to the fullest.

Reverence for Life

When we become aware of the preciousness of our own life, we become aware of the preciousness of other lives, too, and are thankful for each encounter of every day. Thus opens up the realm of praise.

"Thank you for this day," Rissho Kosei-kai members often say in greeting each other, palms pressed together in reverence. We are grateful for the day, grateful for every encounter of the day.

We are granted life in a truly wonderful world, yet how often do we realize this? Our daily greeting of thanks for the day, offered in a spirit of worship, helps to gradually impress on us the significance of our existence and the marvels of the world in which we live. This gesture of greeting is an acknowledgment of the preciousness of the life before us, a sign of respect for the person we are greeting. Our reverence is reciprocated in the same way by the person we are greeting. This makes us aware that the life of the person before us and our own life are equally precious.

Kyoto's Sanjusangendo, famous for its 1,001 statues of the "Thousand-Armed Kannon," is the main hall of the Rengeo-in, a temple dedicated to the Lotus Sutra. The multiple arms of Kannon (Avalokiteshvara) represent the diverse ways in which that bodhisattva saves us from the trials and tribulations of human existence. The two arms at the center of each figure are raised, palm to palm, in the gesture of reverence, demonstrating the bodhisattva's respect for us. It also expresses the bodhisattva's entreaty for the revelation of the buddha-nature within each of us.

Seldom do we recognize the preciousness of our own lives. Even less often do we show reverence for our own being. But doing so should be an important part of our existence.

I am a buddha, you are a buddha

This talk of reverence brings to mind the bodhisattva Never Despise in the Lotus Sutra. The Zen priest Ryokan (1758–1831), famous for his calligraphy and poetry, wrote this about the bodhisattva Never Despise: "A *biku* needs to do nothing but practice what the bodhisattva Never Despise did." A *biku* is a Buddhist cleric. Most likely, Ryokan wanted to say that, more than any other kind of training, a priest's time and energy are best spent in emulating the bodhisattva Never Despise.

The bodhisattva Never Despise showed his reverence for everyone he met by declaring, "You will become a buddha." For those who were not aware of the preciousness of their own lives, these words were simply bewildering. They became angry. "Don't talk such nonsense," they cried. Some even threw stones at him.

All people are enlightened by the recognition of the Truth and the Dharma. By telling people, "You will become a buddha," the bodhisattva Never Despise was urging them to recognize the Truth and the Dharma and awaken to the preciousness of their own existence. By calling on others in this way, we can help them to reach enlightenment.

Once you realize how important your own life is, it becomes obvious that the lives of others are equally precious. You are grateful for all things and are able to express sincere thanksgiving. This is how we can build a world of mutual respect, a world in which I am a buddha and you are a buddha.

Although we tend to be self-centered much of the time, deep inside us is the wish to live in harmony with all things, to respect all things. By devotedly continuing our practice of pressing our palms together in reverence to one another, our respect and reverence for others will gradually grow to encompass our family, friends, community, and workplace, so that in each situation we can live in harmony, doing our best. This is the way, I believe, that we can change the world into a warm, cheerful, and welcoming place overflowing with the joy of life.

Worship the Buddha, worship human existence, worship all things. What a wonderful world this is! Only human beings are capable of worship, but this does not mean that we are in any way superior to other living things. Still, we should be grateful that we have been given life as human beings who are capable of worship.

Our words invoking the Lotus Sutra, *Namu Myoho Renge-kyo* (I take refuge in the Sutra of the Lotus

Flower of the Wonderful Law), express our oneness with the universe, our oneness with the great life of the universe. *Namu* means to make oneself nothing, to give one's whole being to the Buddha, which is, after all, to give oneself over to the Truth and the Dharma. Recite those words with reverence, and you will overflow with the joy of being supported by the eternal life.

CHAPTER 3
SALVATION THROUGH BUDDHISM

For True Salvation

What is the essence of faith? If we can properly recognize this, all our anxieties, all our sufferings, will disappear.

Our lives are full of suffering and pain, as well as joy and pleasure. All of us suffer setbacks of one kind or another. It is natural to wish for succor when we experience conflict with the people around us or when we are ill. Many people turn to God and the Buddha for help. In fact, people generally turn to religion in the hope that faith will rescue them from the sufferings of this world.

It is only human to want to be saved, so there is no need to deny this wish. Wanting to be happy may seem selfish, but the desire for individual happiness at its root is linked to the broader wish for the happiness of all humankind. For those of religious faith, succor and peace are to be found in worshiping or taking refuge in the focus of their devotion. When suffering seems unbearable, appealing to God and the

Buddha alleviates our pain. With the focus of devotion before us, it is a little easier to realize that we have not been as considerate of others as we could be, that we have not tried hard enough, that perhaps we have complained too much. Our interest shifts from material desires to the wish to live as God and the Buddha would have us live.

Since human existence is often self-centered, people usually turn to religion when a problem is too hard to resolve by oneself. "I can't solve this," one thinks, yet the desire to do something about it is strong. It is at those times that we turn to the faith we have so long ignored. Suddenly we see that we are enabled to live through the good graces of others, and our life changes from being self-centered to being dedicated to serving others.

We turn to religion in the hope that it will save us from financial reverses, cure our illnesses, mend our relationships, and fulfill our everyday wishes. But religion is more than just a shelter for those in trouble. Even the happiest person, with a close and caring family and wanting for nothing, can turn to religious faith in the search for a life of true value. Shakyamuni sought the salvation of all people. He left a life of affluence in the quest for a meaningful existence. That is what religion, or faith, is really all about.

In his *Rissho ankoku-ron* (Treatise on the Establishment of the True Dharma and the Peace of the Nation), Nichiren (1222–82) warned against turning to religion only to serve one's immediate wants: to become rich, to be cured of an illness, to bring peace to a family in turmoil, to resolve fears for the future. Rather, he said, one should "take refuge in the One Virtue of the True

Vehicle," which means to give oneself totally to the
Lotus Sutra, the foremost of the Buddha's teachings.

We have so many wants and desires, and are quick
to ask for this and that. What we really need to do is
discard this small and narrow faith in order to establish a firm faith in the Buddha Dharma, the Buddha's
Law. That is what Nichiren was talking about, and
what he meant was to live in accordance with the Truth
and the Dharma that Shakyamuni discovered through
his enlightenment.

To abide by the Buddha's teachings is to willingly
give oneself up to a force that transcends the individual self. True salvation can be attained only through
true faith. The Rissho Kosei-kai Members' Vow refers
to this in the words "We . . . recognize in Buddhism
the true way of salvation." The first step to this recognition is to discard a faith that is founded only on personal wants and return to the essence of Buddhism.

Buddhist awareness

What is true salvation? To know true salvation is to
understand the concept of the one great cause of the
buddhas' appearance in this world and open one's eyes
to the Buddha-knowledge as explained in chapter 2 of
the Lotus Sutra, "Tactfulness," which states: "Why
[do I] say that the buddhas, the world-honored ones,
only on account of the one [very] great cause appear
in the world? Because the buddhas, the world-honored ones, desire to cause all living beings to open
[their eyes] to the Buddha-knowledge so that they may
gain the pure [mind]."

"The one [very] great cause" refers to the buddhas'
one great reason, their most important reason, for ap-

pearing. The passage goes on to refer to the buddhas' desire to show all living beings the Buddha-knowledge, to cause them to apprehend the Buddha-knowledge, and to cause them to enter the way of the Buddha-knowledge. The buddhas' one great reason, however, can be summarized as the opening of one's eyes to the Buddha-knowledge, or the Buddha's wisdom.

The buddhas came into this world in order to open our eyes to the Buddha-knowledge. The most important thing for us is to achieve this Buddhist awareness. The phrase "open [their eyes]" suggests that the Buddha-knowledge is something we already have but are unaware of. To put it another way, everyone has the Buddha-knowledge.

Another phrase that appears in the "Tactfulness" chapter is "the true aspect of all things." To have the Buddha-knowledge, or the Buddha's wisdom, is to be able to see the real aspect of all things. What is the reality of the world, of human existence, as seen through the Buddha-knowledge? In the eyes of the Buddha-knowledge, nothing is ever the same; everything is undergoing constant change. As we know, this is the law of transience. To open our eyes to the Buddha-knowledge within ourselves is to understand the law of transience.

When we look at the world with the Buddha-knowledge, we see that nothing exists in and of itself. Instead, everything is dependent on everything else. We coexist in a relationship of mutual support and dependence. Each part of the whole is thus linked with the other parts in one great life. This interdependence can be described as the state of "nonself." Transience and nonself are the true aspect of this world. To attain

Buddhist awareness is to become aware of these truths, particularly the truth of transience.

How to see

The essence of Buddhism is to see the world as it really is. Very often we become so mired in our worries and pain that we fail to see the reality before us. We would not suffer nearly so much if we would only look at what is really there.

It is not easy to see with Buddhist awareness. Sometimes we think we are seeing the whole when actually we are seeing only a part. We cannot see things correctly when we are looking through self-centered eyes. What then is the right way to look at things? The first step is to observe calmly and objectively, to look from all sides so that we can see the whole. The next step is to go beyond appearances to perceive the reality within.

We all have the Buddha-knowledge within us. All we need to do is observe without prejudice. We need to see how things change, how everything is interconnected. We will then be able to see clearly that we ourselves, those around us, and in fact all things are undergoing constant change. We will see suffering become happiness, conflict become harmony. We will also see that everything is given life by everything else, that nothing exists without being dependent upon something else. Finally, having seen that all is transient and interdependent, we need only to accept this reality as it is.

Right view is given as the first part of the Eightfold Path. To have right view is to see things correctly, and that is to recognize the Truth and the Dharma, the law of transience. Buddhism begins with seeing things as they are. We must look fully on the pain, joy, pleasure, and sorrow of our daily lives—and look, too, at nature as it is. The sun rises and sets; flowers bloom and fade. To see is the starting point of the awareness of transience, and from seeing only the superficial, we advance to seeing the inner being. Life becomes continuous suffering only when we view things with fixed, preconceived ideas, denying the constant change that is really there and believing that we alone are right.

To recognize the law of transience is to see with the Buddha-knowledge, which is to see things as they truly are. That is the way to resolve our troubles and find true salvation.

Overcoming Poverty, Illness, and Conflict

If we do not know the law of transience and are not aware of the preciousness and wonder of life, there is no true salvation.

During Rissho Kosei-kai's first twenty years Japan was struggling to recover from its defeat in World War II. People wanted more than anything else to be relieved from poverty and illness, and from disharmony and conflict within the family. Religious faith offered hope, and Rissho Kosei-kai worked to offer salvation from poverty, illness, and conflict through the Buddha's teachings. Many people did find relief from such travails in the Lotus Sutra.

Now, however, it is time to stop and reconsider.

Have we found true happiness? Have we achieved true salvation?

Recognizing the Truth and the Dharma can relieve our suffering. This means acknowledging that all is transient and awakening to the wonder and value of life. True salvation cannot be attained without an awareness of the Truth and the Dharma and the preciousness of life. Poverty and wealth are relative concepts. We judge whether we are poor or rich by comparing ourselves with our neighbors. Such comparisons become meaningless, however, when we recognize the Truth and the Dharma and the value of our lives. Recognize the dignity and absolute value of your own existence, and you will realize that there can be no comparison with others. You will become sincerely grateful simply to be alive, and poverty will no longer be an issue.

Illness is difficult to deal with. It can be cruel and debilitating. But illness also opens your eyes to the value of your life. When you are sick, you suddenly realize what is most important in life. Of course, nothing is better than good health. Yet many people, when they fall ill, rediscover the Buddha's compassion and are grateful for it.

You can empathize with those who are ill when you have been sick yourself. You know their pain and can share their suffering. When you are in a hospital bed, you become aware of the warmth and caring of family and friends. You awaken to the emotions and thoughts of the doctors and nurses upon whom you depend. You recognize that to fall ill is to know the Buddha's compassion.

Conflict, with those around you or within your own family, arises because you lose sight of the preciousness of one another's existence. Conflict is the clashing of egos that deny the human dignity of others. You cannot see the dignity of other lives when you fail to recognize the preciousness of your own life. Know that your own life is precious, and you will realize that others are equally precious, not simply other people but all life. Conflict becomes impossible. Where conflict exists, joy vanishes. Deep down, we all want to have friendly relations with everyone else.

In today's world, having a certain amount of money is essential. We have to eat; we need clothing. Sad to say, our excessive desire for these essentials of life is a source of suffering. Salvation comes through realizing that all is transient, that all life is precious. With this awareness, we can gain the wisdom and strength to overcome any kind of suffering, including poverty, illness, and conflict.

Steep yourself in suffering

Asked, "How can I be saved from suffering?" the Chinese Zen priest Chao-chou Ts'ung-shen (778–897) is said to have replied, "You must suffer as long as you live." At the core of this seemingly cruel response is reassurance, for Chao-chou is telling us, "I will suffer with you to the bitter end."

We all want to be more flexible and adaptable, but we tend to insist on having our own way, becoming inflexible. When our lives are stable and uneventful, we seldom feel the need to reflect on ourselves, much less change our ways. Suffering offers the chance for major change. Chao-chou's admonishment to continue suffering is meant to open our eyes to the opportunity that suffering gives us to know the Truth and the Dharma and to change the very essence of our being. At the same time, he is teaching us how important it is to know what it means to overcome suffering.

I believe there is a clue here as to how best to deal with the pain of poverty, illness, and conflict. We may not find instant relief from our suffering, but those who awaken to the preciousness of life are able to accept all further suffering with sincere thanksgiving. We learn to look on the bright side. For example, the impoverished may bemoan the cost of feeding the family, but at the same time find renewed energy to work hard precisely because there is a family, a precious family, to support.

Of all human endeavors, recognizing the preciousness of life is the most important. Our goal is not to rid ourselves of suffering as experienced through poverty, illness, and conflict but to take advantage of the opportunity suffering gives us to begin a life of faith founded upon the Buddha Dharma. We can overcome any kind of suffering once we recognize the Truth and the Dharma to which Shakyamuni was enlightened and awaken to the dignity of all life. True salvation is achieved when each individual awakens to the law of transience, recognizes the preciousness of his or her life, and learns to respect the dignity of all life.

Two types of people

There seem to be two types of people: the unhappy person living in the midst of happiness and the happy person living in the midst of unhappiness. The former is the type who has no wants and yet grumbles about what he or she perceives to be lacking in life. On the surface, this kind of person seems to have everything anyone could ever want, but inside, he or she is unhappy, seeing only the negative side of things. The latter type of person is burdened by great unhappiness and yet is able to seek out the small pleasures of life.

Life is full of suffering, but those who can find pleasure in the little things of life will find the shortcut to true happiness. Superficial trappings do not determine a person's happiness. The person who can give thanks in the midst of trials and tribulations is the truly happy person. In contrast, the person who gives no thanks is truly unhappy, no matter how wealthy he or she may be.

Happiness depends on the way we look at things. Japanese people today have a rich material life, but they have lost the sense of thanksgiving that is essential to attaining true happiness. In the Dhammapada, Shakyamuni says, "There is no greater happiness than to be free of sickness; there is no greater treasure than to know sufficiency." No matter how wealthy we may be, if we are not satisfied we will want more and more and will know no peace. That is why the greatest treasure is to be satisfied with what we already have.

Live each day in thanksgiving, and you will be able to tackle life with initiative and a positive attitude. Live each day with dissatisfaction, and you will become passive and negative. Each of us has been given a uniquely valuable life. Let us live not in gloomy dissatisfaction but in glorious thanksgiving.

The Causes of Suffering: Greed, Anger, and Ignorance

If we are ruled by greed, anger, and ignorance, we cannot see the preciousness of life. For the individual to live, for those around him or her to live, and for society to live—this is the way to make the most of precious life, to experience joy, and to fulfill the Buddha's prayer.

Who does not want to live in complete freedom? I believe attaining this deep-seated wish is the key to happiness. How often have we been convinced we are right? How often have we insisted this or that should be exactly thus and so? Usually this happens when we are in conflict with someone and are full of anger. Greed and anger drive us to think and act foolishly. Nothing could be further from true freedom.

Buddhism calls greed, anger, and ignorance the three poisons. They represent the defilements that curtail our freedom. Greed involves always wanting more, never being satisfied. Desire is a natural part of all life, but it becomes a hindrance when carried to the extreme of wanting everything for oneself. It is not limited to the desire for things. The self-centered desire to control people is also a form of greed. Buddhism describes such people as hungry spirits who dwell in one of the six realms of transmigration, always hungry, never satisfied. There is no limit to human greed, and so we become like starving devils.

Anger is born of displeasure and breeds conflict and disharmony. The angry person is like a soul plunged into hell, a place of endless suffering. When we are overtaken by anger, we lose sight of everything else. We find ourselves alone, convinced we are surrounded by enemies—even though human life is premised on interaction with others. The suffering we undergo in this state of mind is like being in hell itself.

Ignorance is the state of being blind to the Truth and the Dharma. Because we fail to understand the law of transience, we confront everything impulsively, which only deepens our pain and suffering. The person who acts in this way has lost the capacity for human reason and is like an animal.

Suppose two people must share two rice balls, one big and the other small. Greed is wanting to have the big rice ball. When one of the two people reaches for the big rice ball, the other person is angered. The person of conscience has self-control and is satisfied to make do with the small rice ball. The ignorant person, however, cannot give up on having the big rice ball and tries to take it away from the second person. This results in conflict, and later a sense of shame arises.

We create our own pain, just as we create our own joy and happiness. Be the first to reach for the small rice ball. This will please the other person, who later will be equally willing to give way.

Being thankful for desire

If we look back on our lives, we are sure to be dismayed by how foolish we have been. Yet our earthly desires, as represented by greed, anger, and ignorance, are an integral part of our lives. We want to eat, sleep, work, live a happy life, and be recognized by others. These desires are what keep us alive. We should not trouble other people, but ultimately we are beings that always trouble someone simply by our own existence. It is the pain we feel at causing trouble to others that forces us to look at ourselves with remorse. Remorse exposes our foolishness, and recognizing this foolishness is a step in our spiritual growth. Recognizing our own foolishness is of great importance.

It is often assumed that Buddhism denies all desire, but that is not so. Wanting to work hard to keep our families comfortable is one kind of desire. Our endeavors to fulfill this desire have a positive effect on society, so in that sense desire is an important driving force in the world. Were we to lack all desire, we would never feel compelled to work for others. Life would become meaningless. The Zen master Dogen said that the life and death of this world represent the life of the Buddha. So our desires—our wants and delusions—are part of the life of the Buddha. We seek the enlightenment of the Buddha in order to cope with our desires. Both our greed and our attempts to grapple with greed are an integral part of the Buddha's life and give meaning to our lives.

It behooves us, then, to concentrate on the here and now, to throw ourselves wholeheartedly into the task at hand. Our motivation may be a little self-centered, but our dedication drives things forward, and that eventually ties in to giving to others. Our desires must be controlled. It is dangerous to pursue them without regard for the way they may affect others. To live is the most important thing. But happiness cannot be attained by concentrating on one's own life alone. Human joy—and the Buddha's prayer—is that we live, those around us live, and all of society lives.

The fountain of wealth within oneself

In the midst of suffering, our overwhelming desire is for relief. More than anything else, we want to be free of pain and anguish. If only we could live without any pain, we think. But if we shift our perspective, we see that in living through the suffering we undergo as a result of greed, anger, and ignorance we experience spiritual growth. People all around us have discovered, through suffering, the three poisons in themselves and begun living lives grounded in the Truth and the Dharma. These people have not been overcome by their troubles; in fact, they are grateful for the burdens that have been placed on them. "It is because I suffered so," they say, "that I am what I am today."

Giving thanks for suffering may seem to run counter to all logic, but the Buddha's teachings make such gratitude possible by showing us the causes of our suffering and guiding us to look within ourselves. Perceived in this way, everything that happens to us is like a sermon from the Buddha. Life becomes full of joy and we are saved.

Consider the woman whose husband is living with another woman and has not come home for many years. Surely jealousy and anger will twist her heart. But the forsaken wife who knows the Buddha's teachings will accept even this as a gift from the Buddha. It is within us all to make a complete about-face and accept whatever may happen with calm thanksgiving. Anger only increases one's pain. Even as she suffers, the betrayed wife may realize that the source of her pain is her own unkindness to her husband. Realizing this, she is freed of pain and is able to wish in all sincerity for her husband's happiness.

Suffering is part of the human condition. Many are the times we are overcome by defeat and failure. That is life; that is the world of transience. However great our pain, however humiliating our suffering and shame, we feel because we live. It is all too easy to separate things into good and bad. We cling to our illusions. But the only way to find true happiness and freedom is to recognize that everything is a gift from the Buddha.

Our illusions and attachments blind us to the reality of the inner self. If we break through the illusions and attachments to dig deep into the inner self, we will discover a rich fountain of wisdom and compassion. This fountain will enrich our lives and make us free. It is the Buddha who first discovered this wonderful fountain and who teaches us now how to discover it for ourselves.

Happiness can be achieved now

Shakyamuni teaches us that everyone has the ability to recognize the Truth and the Dharma. We have the potential to attain the Buddha-knowledge and open the eye of wisdom within ourselves. Yet even though we should be able to overcome any kind of suffering, we usually balk when we are confronted by a serious problem, convinced that we will not be able to cope.

If we recognize the Truth and the Dharma revealed to us by Shakyamuni, we can resolve any difficulty. Every one of us has this ability, but it is up to each individual to strive to realize its potential. Since the ability to recognize the Truth and the Dharma is innate, in a sense we have already attained salvation. The problem is that we seldom realize this. Unaware that we are already saved, we complain, "Why do I have to suffer so much? Why do I have so many troubles?"

The Buddha appeared in this world to save all humanity. That means salvation for you and for me. When we recognize and accept the law of transience, we learn what a blessing it is just to have been born. Suffering and pain arise from our ignorance of the law of transience. Upon awakening to this fact, our complaints are transformed into thanksgiving and we are instantly saved. Everyone is saved—the difference lies only in whether or not we realize it.

The Avatamsaka Sutra tells us that the wisdom of the Buddha is innate not only in human beings but in all living things. Only our attachments and delusions prevent us from seeing the wisdom that is within ourselves. If we rid ourselves of our attachments and delusions, we will at once discover the same wisdom as the Buddha. These are heartening words that should give us all courage.

Salvation here and now

The famous seventeenth-century poet Matsuo Basho wrote this haiku:

The cicada sings, unaware that it is soon to die.

Basho used the cicada as a metaphor for the brevity of human existence.

It is generally assumed that if only we make the effort, we will someday find true happiness. But we need to find happiness right now. There is not enough time to prepare for the future. The world is changing every moment, so there is no knowing what will happen tomorrow, let alone next month or next year. No one knows what the future holds. That is why we need to find happiness here and now. The way to do that is to recognize the law of transience.

Accept that all is constantly changing, and strive to live in a way that seems good to you and to others. You will then find that your worries vanish and you can be truly happy. It is not necessary to strive for years and years. Happiness need not be a future reward, but can be a reality in the present.

The Zen master Hakuin (1686–1769) cites an experience similar to the one recorded by Basho. Hearing a cricket chirping under a rain-drenched rock, Hakuin suddenly recognized the truth of the Buddha's teachings, and his doubts about the Lotus Sutra were instantly erased.

Recognize the law of transience, and your dissatisfaction with life will be transformed into joy and thanksgiving. You will find immediate happiness and will be able to express sincere gratitude for even the worst trouble and suffering. You will be grateful for things as they are.

Be Grateful for Everything

When we become aware of the preciousness of life and the wonder of having been born human, we can perceive our being alive and the most ordinary, everyday things as sermons of the Buddha.

We should give thanks for the life we have received, for having been born as human beings and for having encountered the teachings of the Buddha. There is much to be grateful for. If we realize this, we will be able to be thankful for everything.

Religion teaches us how we should live. With all that has been bestowed on us, it behooves us to live to the fullest. Too often, we seek quick relief in religion. Faith, we mistakenly assume, can make us rich or cure our illnesses. But it is in the ordinary things of everyday life that we will find the true blessings of our faith.

Consider what a miracle it is just to be alive. How wonderful that is! Being able to give thanks for ordinary things helps us to accept things just as they are, even when we are suffering. The mere fact that we have life is enough to fill us with joy. And the lives of others are just as much a miracle as our own existence. We live and are sustained by others. The Buddha's teachings awaken us to the wonder and mystery of the here and now. Our happiness or unhappiness is determined by whether or not we have had the opportunity to become acquainted with the Buddha's teachings. Our recognition of the Truth and the Dharma or failure to do so will determine whether we experience happiness or its opposite.

We believe we are unhappy because we are poor or because we are ill. But happiness is not so simple a matter. The energy to live is generated by our encounter with the Buddha's teachings, our acceptance of the Truth and the Dharma, and our awakening to the wonder of life. Our faith teaches us that these are the sources of true happiness.

No matter how affluent we may be, no matter how good our health, without knowledge of the Truth and the Dharma there can be no genuine happiness. The greatest joy is to be found in the Buddha's wisdom, in the Buddha-knowledge that is inherent in us. The Buddha watches over us and protects us. Knowing this we can be cheerful, grateful for the life we have received. That is the essence of salvation.

Give thanks even for rain

We judge even the weather to be good or bad. "It's a nice sunny day today," we say, or "What fine weather we are having." It is true that our spirits rise when we look up at a bright blue sky. When it is raining, on the other hand, we feel depressed and complain about the bad weather.

As the law of transience tells us, nothing in the world remains the same from one moment to the next. It is therefore only to be expected that the weather will also change: cloudy one day, rainy the next; windy today, calm tomorrow. It is in the natural order of things for the weather to change. It makes no sense for human beings to decide that the weather is "good" or "bad."

When dry days persist during what is supposed to be the rainy season, water levels fall, the rice fields dry up, and water supplies may have to be rationed. Rain quenches our thirst, helps rice and vegetables to grow, and refreshes the earth on which we make our home. Of course, excessive rainfall or severe drought can cause great harm to both people and crops. We need to be prepared for such events, but at the same time we need to learn to give thanks equally for both rain and clear skies. The sun, clouds, rain, and wind all contribute to our lives, and for that we should be grateful. Expressing our thanks is the way to lead lives filled with joy and pleasure.

Live with joy

The ancient Zen master Kaiki was given that name because he found pleasure in everything. The Japanese word *kaiki* means general pleasantness. When the weather was good, Kaiki gave thanks for being able to work outdoors. When it was rainy, he was grateful that he had time to read. Kaiki lived at a remote mountain temple. When a visitor came by, he was pleased to hear news of the outside world; when a day passed in silence, he rejoiced that he could meditate in peace. How wonderful is this ability to see the good side of everything; what a good way it is to live.

Most of us resent people who drop by unannounced when we are busy. How much more would we be able to enjoy life if we could learn to be grateful for such precious encounters, whether or not they suit our convenience at a particular moment. Think about how wonderful it is to enjoy the food we eat, to be able to move our bodies as we wish, to enjoy conversations with others, and to sleep well at night. These minor, everyday pleasures bring joy to our lives.

There is so much to be grateful for: being able to watch our children grow up and mature; learning the lessons of our mistakes; enjoying a brief glimpse of a beautiful wildflower by the road; knowing we have a family that cares about us. The world around us is always changing. Therefore every encounter is a new pleasure to savor. When we realize this, we can find lasting happiness.

If we want to be happy right now, we need only give thanks for everything in our lives. A simple change of perspective can leave us filled with joy. Happiness is possible in the here and now. A life of gratitude is a life that is worth living, a life in which salvation is attained.

The Sublime Prayer

To wish for all humanity to attain true happiness, and to live in accordance with that wish: This is the sublime prayer.

In chapter 2 of the Lotus Sutra, "Tactfulness," the Buddha says, "Of yore I made a vow, wishing to cause all creatures to rank equally without difference with me." The Buddha wants everyone to awaken to the Truth and the Dharma—to become a buddha like himself. He has vowed to do this and is determined to fulfill his vow. It happens that the Buddha's vow and humanity's most deep-seated desire are one and the same.

"How can that be?" you ask. "My personal wishes can't be anything like the sacred vow of the Buddha. The Buddha's vow is all-encompassing, while my own wishes are small and insignificant." We are attracted by the Buddha's vow, however, because it speaks to something that dwells deep in our hearts. The Buddha's prayer is everyone's prayer.

Most of us want to live better than other people, to have more possessions than others. Of course the desire for affluence is a selfish one. But even the most self-centered wish originates in a greater, universal desire that is also the source of the Buddha's vow "to cause all creatures to rank equally without difference with me." The Buddhist believer makes four vows: to guide as many people as possible to enlightenment; to rid oneself of all defilements; to learn the Buddha Dharma; and to attain buddhahood. Our goal is to practice the way of the bodhisattva, one who strives for the salvation of others as well as oneself.

In the secular world, we are always competing and comparing ourselves with others. Yet even in the midst of this competition, we all share the desire to live in harmony and peace with other people. That is why it feels satisfying to be nice to someone, why we find such pleasure in helping others. Our desire to live in harmony with one another is the same as the Buddha's vow to bring happiness to all people. The Buddha's vow speaks to the core of our being because it reflects a wish that is the essence of the human condition. To be able to reach beyond confrontation and conflict to build a world of harmony: That is humanity's prayer.

This "original prayer" can also be seen as our desire to rid ourselves of the preconceived image of an unchanging self in order to live in accordance with the changes of the world; in other words, to live in a condition of nonself. There is no need to lock oneself into a set pattern and declare, "This is the kind of person I am." The self is constantly evolving and changing and has infinite possibilities. This is the way we really are and really want to be.

True salvation lies in the discovery of the genuine prayer that is already within us, for our ultimate de-

sire is the same as the Buddha's. Discovering this desire leads us to true faith and to salvation.

Discovering the genuine prayer within

"Prayer" is a term used by people everywhere, regardless of their religious faith. For Buddhists, prayer is
the same as what is called a vow, and both are at the
core of our being. As I have already said, deep down
all of us want to be friends, all of us want to live in
peace. This hope is rooted deep within us, it is our
prayer and our wish, and we have it whether or not
we are religious. Thus, there is no need to make a special wish or prayer. The wish, the prayer, is already
there within us. All we need to do is make ourselves
aware of it.

Prayer is a personal thing, of course, which spontaneously wells up within us. It is generally assumed
therefore that personal prayer does not really have
the power to move others. But our prayers ultimately
share in the Buddha's prayer and so, I believe, have
the power to change the world. The Buddha dedicated his life to preaching the Dharma. He was energized to do so by wisdom and compassion, by his
vow to awaken all people to the Truth and the Dharma.
Buddhism has passed down this vow through some
twenty-five hundred years, to the present day.

Wishing for the happiness of all

Perhaps the most important wish of humanity is that
all people will attain true happiness. This is such a
lofty goal that it can be called the sublime prayer. To
put it simply, one cannot rejoice in one's own happi-

ness if there is even one unhappy person nearby. This is a simple wish, a simple prayer, that I believe everyone shares.

Shakyamuni was enlightened to the fact that we suffer because we are self-centered in our perceptions. We complain that someone's words have hurt our feelings; we complain that we receive no thanks for doing a favor; we complain that our boss seems unaware of how hard we work. It is precisely these kinds of self-centered thoughts and feelings that disturb human harmony and create suffering.

Discard your little self, get rid of your preconceived ideas, and you will see that everything in this world is constantly changing, that all things are the result of causes and conditions and are born and die, that everything is related, and that all things are one. Once we realize this, we cannot help feeling at one with others, and out of this arises the desire to help and serve others, a sense of caring and compassion.

It is only natural to want to lead a joyful life. After all, each life is unique and precious. But to attain our own joy, we need to stop and carefully examine our innermost being. We think we will be satisfied if only our immediate worries are resolved. But that is not how things work. True satisfaction can be achieved only by conveying the teachings in which we put our faith to as many people as possible. Every religion, in other words, must disseminate its teachings.

The Japanese poet and author of children's stories Kenji Miyazawa (1896–1933) wrote, "There can be no individual happiness until the world as a whole is happy." Those words reflect the Buddha's vow, the sublime prayer. Shakyamuni's desire, his decree, is that each of us become the kind of caring person that Miyazawa had in mind.

Living in Simplicity

As people living in the world today, let us confirm together what is important, what is essential. The basis of a happy life will reveal itself.

The book *Inochi ni deau tabi* (Journey to Life) by the educator Satoru Takeshita includes a poem by the Christian pastor Susumu Kono titled "Which?"

> In Japan,
> Just one bowl of rice
> Seems like nothing.
>
> In India,
> Just one bowl of rice
> Is venerated.
>
> Which brings greater happiness?

Japan is now so affluent that any food left over after we have eaten our fill is thrown away. We forget to be grateful for the food that sustains our lives and waste it without a thought. Far from giving thanks for the food, we complain about its quality!

The poem mentions India, but I believe that is just a symbolic reference, representing any less economically developed nation where even one bowl of rice is precious and worth giving thanks for. How happy can someone really be in an affluent world so full of things? The person who can express sincere gratitude for one bowl of rice is really much happier than the person who is inundated by material wealth. Those of us who live in cities are especially likely to forget the blessings of nature, to forget that we are sustained by God and the Buddha. We become self-centered and are mistakenly convinced that we live by our own will. Before we realize it, we are leading wasteful lives.

The era in which our goal was material affluence is past. Today people are rethinking their values and searching for what will bring them true happiness and make life worthwhile. What is the purpose of human existence? What is the true nature of human beings? This kind of self-examination has always been an essential part of the human condition and will always be so. For a while we forgot this, but today much of the world is looking within, in search of more substantive values.

Since succeeding to the presidency of Rissho Kosei-kai in 1991, I have used the Japanese characters meaning "simplicity" for my first symbolic calligraphy of the new year. Each time I write these characters with my brush, I contemplate the meaning of Buddhism and pray that I, along with my fellow members of Rissho Kosei-kai, will discover the true essence of our humanity. We worship the Eternal Buddha Shakyamuni, but we do not pray for our personal wishes to be granted. Rather, the objective of our worship is to open the eyes of others as well as our own to the Truth and the Dharma that Shakyamuni revealed for us. We strive to awaken to the preciousness of life, to emulate the Buddha by sharing in the suffering of others with compassion and caring, and thereby to give meaning to our own lives.

My annual calligraphy is my prayer that one day all people will awaken to the true essence of our humanity and our faith.

Living in simplicity

We live in an era of increasingly diverse values and lifestyles. It is indeed important to live in the way that best suits one's own character and interests. We do not need to copy others. But we must never stop asking ourselves what is most important. If we lose sight of the essentials of our humanity, we will end up leading selfish, meaningless lives.

Our lives are rich in material things. In fact, we are too rich. All our wishes are fulfilled, and we tend to indulge ourselves in luxury, allowing our selfish desires to take the lead. Are we not overconsuming things that are not truly necessary? When we realize this, it becomes clear that the solution is to lead a simple life, stripped of all unnecessary trappings. "Simplicity" is the watchword of our new era. It is vital, too, for preserving the natural environment. Simplicity means the absence of frills, the reduction of waste. It means a life that is unadorned and plain.

The Japanese word for "simplicity," *kanso*, is written with two characters, one meaning consistent and uncomplicated, the other meaning integral and without waste. Thus the simple life is one that retains the essentials yet avoids wasteful excess. To attain simplicity we must pinpoint what is necessary and rid ourselves of all that is not.

This means clarifying the true meaning of life and

living with that as our ultimate aim and ideal. Once
we know what our goal is, it becomes obvious what
we must do. Examine everything in your life in terms
of its simplicity. Seek out the essentials, and you will
discover the secret to a happy life.

Simplicity for organizations

When a group of people launches a new business or
any other undertaking, the entire group is energized
and motivated. But it is not easy to maintain that high
level of interest. To continue a tradition is to pass on
its basic spirit to younger generations so as to generate
new undertakings. The larger a group grows, however, the more complex its organization becomes and
the more difficult it is to maintain unity of purpose.
Here, too, simplicity is the key.

Rissho Kosei-kai is involved in numerous and diverse activities, from the basic day-to-day practice of
our faith to projects that are directed to society in general and to the achievement of world peace. All these
activities spring from our desire to apply the Buddha's teachings in our daily lives. Everything we do is
important. Still, when an activity is carried on for too
long, it can become a matter of habit rather than an
act of faith, and we can lose sight of its original purpose.

I once said that we should return to the origins of
Rissho Kosei-kai and focus all our activities on dis-
seminating our faith. Our Buddhist practice is aimed
at revealing the Truth and the Dharma to ourselves
and those around us. At its core is our wish for the
happiness of all humanity. Our goal is not to make a
large organization still larger. We must never forget

our original purpose. Each member of Rissho Kosei-kai must keep this in mind as we pursue our many activities and work together to attain our goals. Only in this way will we evolve into an organization that can respond to the needs of our times and one that will furnish the energy for all of us to enjoy worthwhile and fulfilling lives.

Grasping the essence of faith

To lead a life of simplicity is our basic aim. To achieve this, we need to recognize the heart of the Buddha Dharma, the law of transience. Keeping that in mind, let us all reconsider the way in which we practice our faith, the way in which we live each day. Let us stop to think about what is truly important. Simplicity can help us see things in a clearer light. Simplicity can make it possible to repeat again and again those acts that truly reflect our faith.

At times we have to be versatile and apply ourselves in many different ventures. It is equally important, however, that at times we are able to concentrate on just one thing at a time. We need to be able to focus our attention and devote ourselves with unwavering dedication. We must not hurry, but neither should we pause. Once a member said to me that he interpreted my definition of simplicity as the means of grasping the essence of our faith. That is a wonderful way to understand what I want to convey. Each of us may conceive of simplicity in a different way. My hope is that all of us will apply the concept to every aspect of our lives. For those of us of the Buddhist faith, simplicity is the essence of our religious belief—it is at the core of the Buddha's teaching.

CHAPTER 4

A SECOND BIRTH AND
TRUE HAPPINESS

What Makes Life Worth Living

We realize what truly makes life worth living by recognizing the law of transience and reflecting deeply on the fact of having been born as human beings.

We all want our lives to be worthwhile, but deciding what makes life worth living varies from person to person. For some, value is found in work; for others, it may be participation in volunteer activities; and for yet others, it may be a hobby or watching a beloved child develop.

Some say the value of existence is to be found in a life of fulfillment. But value is not easy to define. What we must consider first is the fact that we have been given life in this world. Having acknowledged this miracle, next we should seek what is most important in human existence, that which is common to all humanity. Shakyamuni teaches us that the one and only reason we have been born into this world as human beings is to reveal the Buddha's wisdom within ourselves. To be open to the Buddha's wisdom is to know and understand the law of transience, that everything in the universe undergoes constant change.

By recognizing the law of transience we recognize the wonder of our own lives and the preciousness of each moment of every day. When we understand transience, we can no longer remain idle. This greater consciousness makes us hope to become friends with everyone we meet; it makes us wish to live in harmony with others by bringing out what is best within our own character; it imbues us with joy and the aspiration to attain these hopes.

With this joy in our hearts, life becomes fulfilling and is enriched by boundless possibilities. All this we can achieve by revealing the Buddha's wisdom within ourselves and recognizing the law of transience.

The fulfillment of birth

It is common to speak of a fulfilling life, but how often do we hear about the fulfillment of being born? There is fulfillment, or special meaning, in our birth as human beings. As it happens, we have been born as human beings rather than birds or fish. This is a remarkable thing. Through the constant progress of science, we have learned a great deal about the origins of life and the wonders of existence. But we still do not know where each person's life comes from or where it goes. The most we can say is that God and the Buddha have given us life as human beings.

There are countless life forms in this world, interconnected in a single life system. All of life is precious. To have been given life as human beings is especially important because as human beings we are capable of recognizing the Truth and the Dharma.

None of us remember anything from before we were born. We have no memory of wanting to be born into this world; we do not remember ever making a decision to be born as human beings. We do not recall making any special effort or performing good deeds just so that we would be born as human beings. And yet here we are, members of the human species for no particular reason that we can think of.

The more we contemplate the wonder of existence, the more we are convinced that we must owe our lives to one great being or life force. And since we have been born human, it seems reasonable to think that there must be an important reason for our existence. To live in fulfillment, to be born in fulfillment: The reason for our existence is to encounter the Truth and the Dharma, to recognize and accept the law of transience.

The Lotus Sutra tells us that we are born with the aspiration to save all people, and this aspiration is what leads us to choose to be born as human beings. This is a religious interpretation of the reality of humanity. Our lives undergo drastic change once we recognize that we have this innate wish. "I came into this world because I wanted to," we realize, and this realization fills us with an overwhelming desire to help others. The reason for one's existence and the goal of one's life become clear. The purpose of life is to live for others, to live together in joy and cooperation. Nothing can be more fulfilling.

The True Awakening

We cannot call ourselves truly human just because we have been born human. It is important to awaken to the true significance of human life—to undergo a second birth—by encountering the Buddha Dharma.

We hold dear many things in life: work and position, home and family, good health, and more. Equally dear to many are thoughtfulness and caring, kindness and flexibility. But what really makes having been born worthwhile, what is at the root of our very existence, is the Buddha Dharma, the law of transience. This is what gives meaning to our lives and makes life worth living.

To encounter the Buddha Dharma and recognize the law of transience is in a sense equivalent to being born again. It is when we experience this second birth that our lives as human beings take on special meaning. Of course, we are grateful simply to have been given life in this world. But if we go no further than this physical birth, we are little more than self-centered beings full of the three poisons of greed, anger, and ignorance. The birth of the true human being occurs when this self-centered being experiences the second birth of accepting the Buddha Dharma.

The significance of being born as human beings is to encounter the Buddha Dharma and thereby awaken to what we really should be. For those who put their faith in the Lotus Sutra, this means becoming the kind of person who will recite the *o-daimoku,* "I take refuge in the Sutra of the Lotus Flower of the Wonderful Law." The person who has yet to encounter the Buddha Dharma lives a self-centered life full of greed, anger, and ignorance. In this type of limited life we fret over not having enough money, worry about falling ill, quarrel with others, and otherwise burden ourselves with worry and suffering. But when we encounter the Buddha Dharma we begin to realize that this is not what life should be all about. We realize that we have been ruled by our worries and concerns and have wasted precious time. Having realized our own ignorance, we begin to seek the true essence of human life, and it is at this point that we at last awaken to our own humanity.

Changing course

What happens to someone who has awakened to his or her own humanity? The Buddha Dharma changes our view of things 180 degrees. Our attention shifts from ourselves to others, and we realize that everything and everyone, including ourselves, is sustained by the Truth and the Dharma. Pessimists who see nothing but tears and anguish in this world suddenly realize that they exist in a world of light and joy. People who are convinced that the world contains nothing but hatred and destruction suddenly see that they are enveloped in the love and caring of countless others. People who see the world as a place of confrontation and rivalry suddenly awaken to a world of peace and cooperation. People who are timid and diffident gain self-confidence.

On the other side of the coin, there are those who, once convinced of their own happiness, are forced to acknowledge how fleeting happiness can be. Likewise, there are those who realize that their success is nothing but a mirage. Resentful people, convinced that their pain is someone else's fault, realize that this is a mistaken view and learn to accept everything, whether sorrow and misfortune or joy and happiness, as a lesson from the Buddha.

From this stage, we move to a new plane of awareness where we are able to see that there is a strange and remarkable power driving the whole universe. That 180-degree change of perspective is brought about by our encounter with the Buddha Dharma. And this encounter with the Truth and the Dharma is the most important thing that can happen in life.

Our Mission

We have been placed on Earth by God and the Buddha and have been charged with a mission. Realization of that mission makes life worth living.

The world's population today is estimated to total some 6.7 billion people. Not one of those people was born into this world of his or her own volition. Yet we have been given life as human beings. Why? I have already explained that this is the working of a great power beyond human comprehension. Some people call this power God; some think of it as the Buddha. We have been placed on Earth by this great and wonderful power, but none of us knows what this really means or what our mission in life is.

Shakyamuni was in his mid-thirties when he attained enlightenment. A look at history will show that many of the great people of this world were nearly halfway through life before they awakened to their mission in the world. It therefore seems reasonable to conclude that we too will not know why we have been born until we have had some experience of life with all its vicissitudes.

Chapter 2 of the Lotus Sutra, "Tactfulness,"declares that "the buddhas, the world-honored ones, only on account of the one [very] great cause appear in the world." If we think carefully about this passage, it becomes clear that we too have been made to appear in this world by "the one [very] great cause" in order to realize the Buddha's vow that all living beings be made aware of the true wisdom that he had attained. Those of us who have encountered the Buddha Dharma learn from it and endeavor to convey the Buddha's teachings to others. We have been born into this world to realize the Buddha's vow. That is our mission in life, and we are filled with joy and thanksgiving from the moment that we become aware of it.

The Buddha's spirit, his prayer for this world, is contained in the Lotus Sutra. What is this spirit, this prayer? It is that the world may be transformed into a Pure Land.

The Buddha's decree

After attaining enlightenment Shakyamuni spent the remaining forty-five years of his life traveling far and wide to preach the Dharma. Never did he seek his own peace. By following in his footsteps and concentrating on his words, we can see that his greatest desire was to create a Pure Land in this world.

The Buddha decreed that we who endeavor to follow his Way must strive to build the Pure Land he envisioned. That is his teaching and the mission he entrusted to us. It is our belief that world peace can be achieved through dissemination of the Buddha's teachings. Like the Buddha, we must begin with ourselves. Our ultimate goal is to bring peace to our society, our nation, and the world, but the starting point is our own peace and the peace of our families.

I may seem to be implying that this mission has been given only to those of the Buddhist faith, but that is not so. Rather, we of the Buddhist faith must move to the forefront and follow the Way to achieve world peace. The Buddha's prayer includes all humanity, not just Buddhist believers. To achieve lasting world peace we must start by sharing our awareness of the truth that is universal with all humankind. We must overcome narrow national, ethnic, and religious boundaries. Peace draws closer with every individual who awakens to his or her mission in life.

The Way to Happiness

To realize the preciousness of life, to give thanks for the gift of life, and to devote oneself to serving others: That is the way to happiness.

The road to happiness, the way to a fulfilling life, is to recognize that everything is transient and to realize the wonder of being alive. There can be no true happiness—no matter how healthy we may be, no matter how wealthy or famous—without acknowledging the preciousness of life, without giving thanks for being alive.

There are two requirements for being happy. One is to become someone who can express gratitude. Begin by being thankful for having been born as a human being. Awaken to the value of your life, and you will realize that the lives of others are equally precious. Giving sincere thanks becomes easy and natural. You will find yourself saying thank you for the smallest favor. No ego is involved in the act of thanksgiving. Giving thanks is an act of selflessness that allows us to bond with others, that fills us with the warm glow of happiness. View the events of the day in a Buddhist context, and you will find much to be grateful for. Look inward, feel how the Buddha has given you life, and you will be filled with grateful contentment.

The second requirement for happiness is to give joy to others—to commit yourself to the bodhisattva practice. Begin with the people that you encounter every day. Making someone else happy will make you happy. You will share in each other's joy. If you cannot bring joy into the life of another, you will not find joy in your own life. Begin by thinking of others, and you will discover your own true happiness.

Living the bodhisattva way is easy once you recognize how precious life is. You will find joy in serving others—in fact, serving others is what will make your life worthwhile. Why is happiness to be found by living the bodhisattva way? Because the ultimate satisfaction in life, the epitome of being human, is to forget the self in service to others. Become someone who can give thanks; become someone who can give joy to others: These are the most important factors in finding true happiness.

You can find true happiness and meaning in your

life right here and now. Awaken to the law of transience, be grateful for the life you have been given, and pray that you will be able to bring joy to others. Live every day to the fullest. Each day will be happier and more satisfying than the day before.

"Normal" life and "normal" happiness

A koan is an enigmatic exchange between a Zen master and a disciple that provides a glimpse into Buddhist truths. One of my favorites is the following exchange between the Zen master Chao-chou Ts'ung-shen and one of his disciples.

"Master, what is the first principle of Buddhism?"
"Have you eaten?"
"Yes, Master, I have eaten."
"Did you wash your bowl?"
"Yes, Master, I washed my bowl."
"That is enough."

It is hard to see what lesson is being conveyed in this brief exchange. But in fact there is a very important lesson to be learned here.

What is the first principle of Buddhism? What is the most important thing in Buddhism? When the master asks, "Have you eaten?" he does not want to know if your belly is full. Rather, he wants to know if you have eaten with thanksgiving. To enjoy food, you must be in good health. Do not forget, either, that the food you eat represents the blessings of nature and the hard work of many hands. Eat with thanksgiving for all that your food represents.

The master's next question is "Did you wash your

bowl?" He is asking more than whether you have performed that simple act. He is asking if you have washed your bowl with thanksgiving for the food it contained.

This koan is a lesson in Buddhist thanksgiving. Give thanks for your good health and for the food you eat, and show your gratitude by washing your bowl. This is the essence of Buddhism and pertains to every aspect of daily life.

Give a cheerful reply when you are called; say thank you when someone is kind to you; lend a helping hand when someone needs it. Apply yourself wholeheartedly to the role and to the work you have been assigned. This is what the koan teaches, and this is what pertains to every aspect of life. That is what is "normal" for human existence. Do what is "normal," and you will not only make yourself happy—you will also bring joy to those around you.

Benefit yourself and others

The greatest joy is to give meaning to the lives of others. If we benefit others, we benefit ourselves. This is nothing but the manifestation of the virtues of the Buddha. In other words, both benefiting ourselves and benefiting others are perfected in the virtues of the Buddha. To save ourselves, we must have compassion for others. We must strive to show people the Truth and the Dharma. We know in our innermost being that we cannot be happy with our own salvation if there is no salvation for our families and friends, or indeed for all humanity. That is the spirit of benefiting others, and all of us wish for the salvation of everyone else.

That is why we find such joy and satisfaction in the Buddha Dharma, which shows us the Way to salvation for the self, for others, and for all people. We believe in a Buddhist faith that proclaims salvation for all people and for all that has life. Our goal is to go beyond our individual salvation to save everyone by guiding others to recognition of the Truth and the Dharma. The Buddha lived for the salvation of others. We can do the same and find our deepest satisfaction in serving others, in allowing others to live as we ourselves are allowed to live.

There is a great joy to be had in helping someone else recognize the preciousness of life. I believe this is true for everyone. The laws that nothing has an independent or a permanent self apply to all of us. We all share the same desire to guide another to the shore of enlightenment even before we reach it ourselves. Once we savor the joy of guiding another, we will find ourselves filled with an overwhelming desire to serve. In this way, we achieve a merging of what benefits the self with what benefits everyone. To serve others is what brings us the greatest joy and the deepest satisfaction.

Know Yourself

What is the true self? When we know that, we find true happiness and a sense of worth.

Shortly after Shakyamuni began his preaching journeys, he stopped in a grove of trees on the outskirts of a small village. He was sitting in contemplation when suddenly a group of excited young men disturbed his solitude. One of the young men asked him, "Did you see a young woman come this way?" He went on to explain, "We brought her with us for a picnic in this grove to have a good time, but she stole our jewels and ran away."

The young men were all well dressed and had good manners, but they were forgetting themselves in their anger over their lost valuables. Shakyamuni saw them as full of greed, anger, and ignorance. He quietly asked them, "Which is more important to you, finding the young woman or finding yourselves?"

Suddenly brought back to his senses, one of the youths replied, "I think finding myself is more important." Shakyamuni bowed his head and motioned the young men to seat themselves around him. He then began to preach.

The young men had been fretting and thinking only of retrieving their stolen property, but this just proved how little they realized what was really important. Blinded by their selfish desires, they could not see what was right in front of them. That is why Shakyamuni chided them by saying, "Which is more important to you, finding the young woman or finding yourselves?"

The Buddha's lesson to the young men applies to all of us. We rush hither and yon, our feelings swinging between pessimism and optimism. Like the young men chasing after the young woman, we have lost sight of our real selves. We do not have confidence in our own being. We are not truly independent.

Here is another example of the Buddha's wisdom.

A disciple complains, "Half a year has passed since I entered this temple, but Master, you have taught me nothing."

The master replies, "How strange! I have been teaching you every day."

The disciple should have been observing the master carefully, studying his every word and deed. That is the only way the disciple could become truly independent. Each of us possesses a precious life; we are all unique and irreplaceable individuals. The person who can fully manifest this is the person who has achieved independence. In Buddhism, as in the arts, what ultimately matters is oneself.

We must first know ourselves if we are to achieve our independence. In general, the idea of knowing oneself is considered in a relative context. For example, corporate heads and business executives are fond of quoting the words of the ancient Chinese military strategist Sun-tzu: "To know your enemy as you know yourself assures you of victory in one hundred battles." You cannot achieve victory if you do not know your own power and the power of your enemy. The world of business is one of daily competition. Knowing yourself is essential if you are to compete successfully.

The self of Buddhism, though, has a deeper meaning than the self as we usually think of it. We can define self by a person's title and function—for example, a person's position in a company or role as a parent. These are relative perceptions, however, that can change depending on the circumstances. Buddhism assumes an absolute self that transcends the relative self. Our goal is to know this true self. And the way to know the true self is through recognition of the Dharma.

"To learn the Way is to learn the self"

The Zen master Dogen is known for these famous words about the self: "To learn the Way is to learn the self. And to learn the self is to forget the self." Here, to learn means to follow an example. To learn the Way is to learn from Shakyamuni, to follow the example of Shakyamuni. The Dharma that Shakyamuni imparted to us enables us to learn how we should live. To learn the self is to complete the self through recognition of the Dharma.

To learn the self is also to forget the self. This is not the small self of myself or yourself. Rather, it is the self to which Shakyamuni was enlightened. We tend to perceive the self as a composite of the experiences, knowledge, and personality that we contain within our own being. But the self Shakyamuni discovered is not as small as that.

The Lotus Sutra quotes Shakyamuni as saying, "Now this triple world / All is my domain." The entire universe and everything existing within it is the self that Shakyamuni discovered in his enlightenment. That is the universal and infinite self. In contrast, the self of our being is a self that eventually must disappear. That is what is meant by the phrase "to forget the self."

How, then, can we experience Shakyamuni's infinite self? The first step is to recognize the law of transience. Our individual lives are limited, but when we view our lives in the light of the law of transience, we realize that those lives are part of a greater life cycle of repeated birth and death throughout eternity. Because we are part of this eternal life, our own individual lives are also eternal. The universe is one great life in which all lives are connected. We are therefore one with the universe.

In Buddhism, to know the self is to go beyond the physical and mental individual self to know the self that is one with the great life of the universe—the absolute self that cannot be compared to any other. We glimpse this self when we accept that we live eternal lives and are one with the universe.

All this comes into clear focus when we recognize and accept the law of transience. We are able to see the true self, we become truly independent, and we are truly born the moment we recognize that law.

We can change ourselves

Watching what other people do, we tell ourselves we would never behave that way, viewing ourselves as totally consistent. In truth, however, we shift this way and that in response to the conditions that happen to impinge on us. Even when we wish to follow the Buddha's Way steadfastly, the causes and conditions we meet with stir up the three poisons of greed, anger, and ignorance. Paradoxical though it may seem, we are not so narrow as to do only good. We have the breadth to do evil, too. In short, we have boundless potential for both good and evil. To see oneself this way is to know oneself.

We may judge ourselves by our own narrow yardsticks—concluding, for example, that we are worthless—but that is not all there is to us. Some people, after all, highly approve of those who are always diffident. Thus, we can know ourselves as we truly are only by looking at ourselves holistically, including the way we appear to those around us. By interacting with many people we discover to our surprise that we can do more than we had thought. And with each such discovery we enrich and expand our self-awareness.

We tend to deprecate ourselves, unaware of the value of our own lives, or conversely to think cockily that we can do anything, that no one can outdo us. But human beings are capable of both good and evil. No one in the world can claim that he or she alone is absolutely right; by the same token, everyone has an essential role. That is why it is so important to scrutinize ourselves constantly in the light of the Buddha's teachings.

Realizing our inadequacies

When someone harshly points out one of our personal flaws, most of us tend to react emotionally. But if we can accept such criticism as having allowed us to become aware of another of our inadequacies, it can lead to unexpected joy. If we can reflect that our swift anger at being criticized shows the strength of our ego, criticism becomes the voice of the Buddha, and we can gratefully revere the critic as the agent of self-improvement.

If we can accept the things that happen around us and our encounters with other people with this kind of flexibility, everything and everyone becomes precious. At the same time, we come to understand our own immaturity and foolishness. Honen (1133–1212), the founder of the Jodo (Pure Land) sect of Buddhism, was deemed the wisest man of his time, and yet he referred to himself as "the foolish priest Honen." And Shinran (1173–1263), a disciple of Honen and founder of the Jodo Shin (True Pure Land) sect, called himself Gutoku, or "ignorant bald-headed one." Prince Shotoku, too, characterized himself as "foolish and inadequate." All were saying, in effect, that no matter how highly society evaluated them, they saw themselves as the most foolish of men. In short, they denied themselves. I imagine that they referred to themselves in such self-deprecating terms because the more they studied the Buddha's teachings, the more deeply they felt the inadequacy of their understanding.

We human beings are full of self-centered delusions, but when we take refuge in the Dharma we can efface ourselves. We cease to pride ourselves on our power and stop behaving arrogantly. With gratitude for the life we have been given here and now, we approach each encounter, every day, with humility. And when we come to know our inadequacies, we understand that we are sustained by a great life force that far transcends our petty selves. We realize that we live in the very midst of the realm of the Truth and the Dharma. Realizing the preciousness of this life bestowed upon us, we find the resources to live with serenity and ease. Thus is the realm of self-affirmation revealed.

Putting oneself in order

Shortly before his death Shakyamuni admonished his disciples, "Make the self your light, make the Dharma your light." In other words, rely on yourself and on the Dharma, not on others. And in the Dhammapada he says, "You are the master of yourself, you are your own refuge. You should therefore control yourself even as the wise horse seller controls a good steed." When we seek to control or regulate ourselves, we often receive guidance from our seniors and other mentors, but ultimately we have to do the job ourselves.

Every morning I put my body and mind in order through special exercises. I imagine everyone has his or her own method of self-regulation. Since ancient times it has been taught that ordering one's posture, breathing, and mind is the basis for physical and mental control. For example, when we chant sutra passages morning and night, straightening the spine and breathing deeply, the mind falls naturally into order and we are infused with gratitude for the life we have been given. And when we observe what is going on around us with a firmly grounded body and a calm mind, we can clearly see the law of transience in action.

To put ourselves in order, it is important to control body, speech, and mind. Control of speech is especially important, since that leads to control of our thoughts and actions. For example, the habit of greeting others with the salutation used among Rissho Kosei-kai members, "Thank you for this day," cultivates a sense of gratitude. Even if we do not really feel thankful at first, controlling our words and actions will eventually bring our state of mind into line. The first step is to regulate our physical and mental posture and speak accordingly. It means taking the step of unaffectedly saying, "Thank you for this day." Saying this while bowing the head and placing the palms together in a prayerful attitude not only makes the words truly part of us but also leads in the most natural way to venerating the buddha-nature that we all share.

Removing the Framework of Ego

Just as fog obscures our view, so when we are preoccupied with ego we cannot see things as they are and realize that all people are irreplaceable beings.

I often quote the poem "Playground" from *Inochi ni deau tabi* (Journey to Life) by Satoru Takeshita:

> When I'm playing,
> It feels so small.
> When I'm set to picking up pebbles
>   during morning cleanup,
> It feels so big.

The size of the playground does not actually change, but it seems small to the child at play. When we are told to pick up the loose stones, though, it suddenly seems enormous. This poem by a fourth-grader makes an incisive point, expressing how self-centered our thinking is, how we see things only in reference to ourselves.

Buddhism is a teaching that removes self-attachment. It is when things do not go as we wish that we suffer. If we come to terms with the fact that by nature life is something that does not go according to plan, a broad perspective opens up before us; but if we cling to the desire to make life follow our wishes, our suffering simply deepens. This wish to make everything conform to our wishes is self-attachment. We suffer because we wedge ourselves into the framework of ego. The Truth and the Dharma taught by Shakyamuni remove that framework and make our relationships with others harmonious.

When we are enveloped in mist or fog, we cannot see our surroundings clearly. Likewise, when the mist of self-attachment arises, when we are wrapped in the fog of self-centeredness, we cannot see things as they are. Wide and narrow, deep and shallow, big and small—such comparisons, too, reflect our egocentric view of things. When this egocentrism, this self-attachment, disappears, the things of the world can be seen as they really are.

When we rid ourselves of ego, we can also see others clearly. We realize the folly of competition based on preoccupation with the relative differences between ourselves and others. Realizing that others, too, are irreplaceable beings, we are able to accord them the respect they are due. When this happens, we can all be as one.

Humility is the most important quality for human beings, and it is generated by recognition of the Truth and the Dharma. My dearest wish is for everyone to remove the framework of ego, or self-attachment, and join in a circle of harmony.

Breaking free of egocentricity

Urabon is the Japanese transliteration of the Sanskrit *ullambana*. *Ullambana* can also be translated into Japanese as *token*, written with two characters, meaning to hang or suspend (*ken*) upside down (*to*). Being hung or suspended upside down is certainly painful, but even without going that far we human beings suffer over all sorts of things. *Token* means that everything we see, hear, and think is topsy-turvy.

The reason we see things as inverted is that we think of everything in a self-centered way, under the illusion that we are right. We are, in effect, suspended upside down. This state can also be expressed by the Sanskrit *viparyasa*—error, delusion. The word is translated into Japanese as *tendo*, which also means "with positions reversed," indicating a way of seeing and thinking that is totally in error. For example, if we could accept advice without resistance, we would not suffer; but in reality we find this almost impossible. We misinterpret well-intentioned advice and as a result bring suffering both to ourselves and to those around us.

Self-attachment, or egocentricity, means seeing and thinking about things in reverse order, being bound to a rigid and cramped way of thinking. This is a sign of an impoverished spirit.

The tale of the origin of the festival of Ullambana (known as O-Bon in Japan) symbolizes this spiritual impoverishment. One day, so the story goes, Maudgalyayana, one of Shakyamuni's ten great disciples, wondered how his deceased mother was faring. Meditating on this, he learned that she had fallen into the realm of hungry spirits, suffering ceaseless hunger and thirst. Maudgalyayana, being a devoted son, was dismayed and immediately took her food and water, but as soon as she tried to partake of them, the food and water went up in flames.

After much anguished thought, Maudgalyayana

asked Shakyamuni for help. In response, the Buddha preached the Ullambana Sutra, in which he taught Maudgalyayana to make offerings to the seekers of the Way of the Sangha, or community of disciples, in order to gain his mother's deliverance. Maudgalyayana blamed himself for his mother's plight, reasoning that if he had not existed, his mother would not have committed the sin of clinging greedily to her precious son. It was he who had led his mother astray and caused her to become a hungry spirit, so to save her he himself would have to be saved. He realized that for seekers of the Way to attain enlightenment as soon as possible and spread the Buddha's teaching far and wide would lead to his mother's salvation as well. In other words, he understood that all suffering people, not only his mother, needed to be saved, and that when everyone was saved—and only then—his mother would attain true salvation. When Maudgalyayana reached this understanding, his mother was delivered from the realm of hungry spirits.

When our way of seeing and thinking is topsyturvy, everything becomes painful. That is why it is important to remove the framework of ego so that we can become capable of serving others and seeing everything as it truly is.

Chapter 7 of the Lotus Sutra, "The Parable of the Magic City," contains this verse:

> May this [deed of] merit
> Extend to all [living things]
> That we with all the living
> May together accomplish the Buddha Way!

As this shows, the salvation of all is the goal of the Buddha Way.

Tips for honing selflessness

Greetings are generally regarded as a courtesy, a social and interpersonal lubricant. But there is more to greetings than that; in a broader sense, they represent a means of achieving a state of selflessness that lets us establish empathy and harmony with others.

When we meet others, we can greet them spontaneously because we have forgotten the self. The same applies to the ability to respond clearly and crisply as soon as someone addresses us. When we are preoccupied, we cannot greet or respond to others spontaneously. We modern people, with our strong egos, find it very hard to let go of the self, but exchanging greetings loosens the framework of the ego, allowing us to empathize and thus achieve harmony with others.

The Japanese word for greeting or salutation, *aisatsu*, is originally a Buddhist term. Both *ai* and *satsu* have the sense of approaching or drawing near. In a Buddhist context, *aisatsu* refers to the way a master gauges the extent of a disciple's spiritual endeavor by the way the latter responds when summoned. When the master calls, "You, there!" the way the disciple replies, "Yes," is enough to tell the master whether the disciple is in a selfless state and has a firm grasp of the Dharma.

Interpersonal relations flow as smoothly as water when we exchange greetings frankly and honestly; only the ego blocks us from doing so. When the father of a family does not greet family members of his own accord, for example, it is because he has the fixed notion that it is proper for others to greet him first. Even people who cannot greet others in a straightforward manner really want to do so in their heart of hearts, but pride stands in the way. The inability to utter a simple greeting deprives them of the joy of feeling the heart expand and open up. In this sense, they are suffering.

I feel uncomfortable when I am in an elevator with someone I do not know and we both stand there silently, neither of us acknowledging the other. If, however, I take the initiative and say, "Hello," the other person invariably responds, "Hello," and the atmosphere relaxes. Thus is a certain harmony established.

When we see a flower and spontaneously murmur, "Oh, how pretty," this honest expression of feeling is a kind of greeting. The great potter Kanjiro Kawai once said, "I gaze at the flower, the flower gazes at me." Perhaps it is because we sense the flower's subtle gaze that we look at it. In this way we and the flower exchange greetings; in other words, life resonates with life.

As members of Rissho Kosei-kai, we chant the *o-daimoku*, "I take refuge in the Sutra of the Lotus Flower of the Wonderful Law," daily as a greeting signifying our unity with the universe. This is the most important greeting of all.

Practicing selflessness at home

Pondering whether we cannot somehow break down self-centeredness in the context of daily life, I came to realize that there are several easy ways to do so, and I like to talk about them whenever I have the opportunity. They are amazingly simple.

First, if we think about whether husband and wife,

parents and children, actually say good morning to one another, I imagine we will discover that surprisingly often people do not bother to greet their nearest and dearest. So the first practice is to say good morning to other members of our own family. Since this sets the tone for the day, it is important not to mumble sleepily but to greet one another cheerfully.

In families where people are not in the habit of saying good morning to one another, whoever resolves to do so first should take the initiative. It takes a bit of courage to begin with, but it is good training for divesting oneself of ego. Taking the initiative in greeting others is an important way of breaking down self-centeredness.

Second, we should respond clearly and crisply when someone addresses us. In our dealings with people in the outside world, we automatically respond when addressed, but we should reflect on whether we do so in our own home. When we are self-absorbed we cannot respond pleasantly. We cannot say the simple word *yes* unless we break down self-centeredness. The way someone says yes reveals his or her character immediately. The ideal is to be able to respond in a way that makes everyone around us feel good. If we can respond in this way at home, we will be able to greet people cheerfully and respond clearly wherever we may be. This is the most important way to ensure smooth interpersonal relations.

Third, when you leave the dining table push in your chair, and when you take your shoes off line them up neatly. Doing so braces you mentally and emotionally. If people are taught to do these things from early childhood, they will be able to exercise balance and moderation when they grow up. They will be discriminating, not squandering money or being careless about things. One who can master this skill will not deviate from the right path.

The philosopher and educator Nobuzo Mori advocates these three practices as the secret of education in the home. They have an important impact on character formation and interpersonal relations. These three simple practices make for a peaceful home and agreeable interpersonal relations at work and in the wider society. That is because they break down self-centeredness and promote selflessness.

The ability to say thank you

There is more. The first thing is to be the kind of person who can say thank you when someone does something for you. Developing the habit of expressing thanks in a frank and honest manner eventually translates into the ability to say thank you from the heart. This is something you can do only when you are selfless; it is impossible when ego gets in the way.

The second is to be able to say "I'm fine, thank you" when someone asks how you are. Just a plain "I'm fine" will do, but the response "I'm fine, thank you" expresses the joy of selflessness. *Okagesama de,* a Japanese phrase meaning "thanks to you," which people often use when exchanging greetings, expresses this joy of selflessness. The phrase represents recognition that one owes one's existence here and now to everything in the universe, that one's life is sustained in countless ways. That is why, when someone asks, "How are you?" you should reply from the heart, "I'm fine, thank you."

The third is to be able to say "I'm sorry." No one is perfect; we all make mistakes. When we slip up, we need to be able to say we are sorry frankly. It is when people have committed a blunder that self-pride is most liable to come to the fore. Saying one is sorry is a shortcut to stripping away the ego. Buddhism teaches the importance of self-reflection and repentance. Put simply, saying sorry comes from repentance.

Striving to become someone who can honestly say thank you, "I'm fine, thank you," and "I'm sorry" is an everyday way of stripping away self-centeredness. The Buddha's teachings are found close to home.

Do No Evil, Do Only Good

When greed, anger, and ignorance build up, the Buddha's wisdom is obscured. When the Buddha's wisdom is obscured, we turn toward evil. Turning toward good—the Buddha—let us strive constantly for self-improvement.

Buddhism teaches of an absolute realm transcending good and evil, but in the context of human life we must discriminate between the two. There are various ways of doing this. In Buddhism, good means turning toward the Buddha and endeavoring to improve oneself. Evil means the opposite: turning toward hell and exacerbating the three poisons of greed, anger, and ignorance. This is the broad meaning of good and evil in terms of Buddhist teaching.

Good means seeing the Buddha's wisdom—specifically, seeing the law of transience and obeying it. Thus, ignorance of the law of transience constitutes evil. In the context of our daily lives, good means realizing the preciousness of life and living each day to the fullest, while evil means struggling with others and being ruled by greed, oblivious to the preciousness of life.

The ultimate wisdom, the Buddha's wisdom, is called *prajna*. *Prajna* is inherent in everyone, but when it is concealed we turn toward greed, anger, and ignorance. And when that which has obscured *prajna* is dispelled, we turn toward good and endeavor to improve ourselves. The state of fully revealed *prajna* is buddhahood. It is because *prajna* is not fully revealed that we fall prey to delusion and attachment. Revealing our inherent *prajna* enables us to turn toward good and strive tirelessly.

Begin by avoiding evil

The verse of admonishment of the seven past buddhas in the Dhammapada answers the question, What is Buddhism?

> To do no evil,
> To do only good,
> To purify one's mind,
> This is the teaching of the buddhas.

The verse begins, "To do no evil." In this case, evil means flouting the precepts that human beings should obey, engaging in unethical and immoral acts. Thus, not doing what is evil means first and foremost refraining from doing anything that would give one a guilty conscience. In other words, right living is important.

Buddhism teaches five precepts that we are to observe in daily life: not to kill, not to steal, not to lie, not to engage in sexual misconduct, and not to drink to excess. These are precepts that everyone should observe as a matter of course. Moreover, it is important that we observe them not because we are told to but on the basis of our own judgment. Essentially, evil arises from ignorance of the law of transience, ignorance of the preciousness of life.

The verse continues, "To do only good." Good is that which accords with ethics and morality, as indicated by the terms "goodwill" and "good nature." Religious practices are also taught as forms of good. I am not talking about some rarefied asceticism; the most basic religious practice is to open the eye of the Buddha-knowledge—to see the Truth and the Dharma. In other words, recognition of the law of transience represents good.

The third line, "To purify one's mind," means attaining the precious wisdom of the Buddha by not doing what is evil and by doing what is good. Purity means living in awareness of the law of transience and in obedience to the Truth and the Dharma. Conversely, impurity means exacerbating delusion and attachment and going against the Truth and the Dharma.

Finally, by not doing what is evil and by doing what is good, strictly observing what should be observed, we gain wisdom, leave behind delusion and attachment, and attain the realm of the Buddha. As the verse says, "This is the teaching of the buddhas."

We should note that the verse begins by warning against doing what is evil. When we resolve to do what is good, the first thing we need to do is stop doing what is evil, such as behaving in ways that violate the five precepts. That means resolving to cease our bad habits from this day forward and then doing what is good. The first two lines of the verse indicate the proper order of self-purification.

Without haste and without pause

Accomplishing anything requires perseverance. Even when we resolve not to do what is evil, we cannot keep it up. It is important to reflect on our failure as often as it takes and resolve to try again. Sometimes it is painful to persevere, but if we try to escape that pain partway through we can never taste enjoyment. As we persevere, pain turns into enjoyment. Discovering that enjoyment in the course of persevering enables us to keep going. For example, many people say they find it difficult to perform sutra recitation every morning and evening. At first this would be hard for anyone, I imagine. Sometimes, tired at the end of a busy day, we find sutra recitation burdensome. But as we persevere, day in day out, little by little we begin to find sutra recitation gratifying, and when that happens we feel unsettled if we skip it, or as if we have forgotten something important. Sutra recitation becomes an indispensable part of our day. Thankful to be able to perform sutra recitation daily, we find that we can persevere naturally. In short, the key to perseverance is a sense of enjoyment and thanksgiving.

There is a passage from the *I Ching* (Book of Changes) that I have made my motto: "The movement of heaven is full of power. The superior man never slackens in perfecting the self." "Never slackens" means striving of one's own initiative and without pause: in other words, constant endeavor. I paraphrase this as "without haste and without pause." "Perseverance is power," as the saying goes. Perseverance in even the smallest things greatly empowers us over time. Repeating the basics is crucial in all things.

Persevering in the endeavor not to do what is evil and to do what is good, without pause and with enjoyment and thanksgiving, purifies our hearts and minds and brings us both a sense of the worth of life and happiness.

CHAPTER 5

TILLING THE FIELD OF THE HEART

The Role of a Buddhist

Tilling the field of the heart is the basis of Buddhism, and a key element of "the age of life." It is this that brings about peace of mind and peace in the world.

The phrase "the age of the heart" first came into use back when Japan was beginning its period of rapid economic growth. It was intended to emphasize the value of the spirit, warning against the notion that satisfying material needs would lead to happiness. I think people felt the urge to focus on spiritual affluence when they realized that although they had, if anything, an overabundance of material things, something was missing—that they could not gain true satisfaction this way.

The spirit has always been important to people, whether or not they are materially blessed. Enriching the heart is the basis of life for us Buddhists. On reflection, however, we realize that while the dimension of the spirit is important for a fulfilling life, physical as well as mental and emotional health is important and that enriching our living environment is also necessary. Buddhism teaches that body and mind are one. The two are inextricably linked. Buddhism does not hold that the mind is superior to the body.

Buddhism sees the importance of the mind as extending to its vessel, the body, and also to the environment. Therefore I prefer to emphasize the immutable importance of what I call "the age of life"—the importance of living in a way that enhances healthy living—which includes such concepts as the age of the heart and the importance of body and mind.

In 1998, the sixtieth anniversary of Rissho Kosei-kai, I announced the overall objective of "each and every one of us tilling the field of the heart." This reflects the vow of the Buddha and the spirit of Rissho Kosei-kai at the time of its founding. The state of Japan and the world at the end of the twentieth century has brought home to us the importance of tilling the field of the heart.

In 1996 I visited Israel, where I discussed the Middle East peace process with Christian, Jewish, and Muslim leaders. The following year I visited Jordan in February and Bosnia in September, exchanging views on conflict resolution and the peace process with many religious leaders. Over the past several years I also had many opportunities to meet and engage in dialogue with Japanese religious leaders.

All this made me aware of the importance of efforts to prepare a conducive climate and enter into various agreements in order to resolve conflict and build peace. At the same time, I was keenly aware that such measures are not the way to a fundamental solution;

that since it is human beings who cause conflict and war and human beings who build peace, there can be no world peace, no fundamental resolution of conflict, unless and until peace is built in the hearts of individuals. I also felt the great hope placed in Buddhism and Rissho Kosei-kai. I realized more than ever that Rissho Kosei-kai exists to work for world peace and true personal happiness.

I feel strongly that we who take the Lotus Sutra as our central scripture, as members of a Buddhist organization, are called upon to reveal the essence of Buddhism and demonstrate true Buddhism to the world. In short, our role as members of a Buddhist organization is to till the field of the heart—in other words, to enhance our own lives. This, I believe, will lead not only to world peace but also to peace of mind and true *joie de vivre*. That is why tilling the field of the heart is our great goal and the basis of living as members of a Buddhist organization and as Buddhists.

Returning to the original spirit

The ancient Chinese calendrical cycle of "ten stems and twelve branches" takes sixty years to complete. The sixtieth year, when the cycle returns to its starting point, thus signifies both a return to the "beginner's spirit" and a fresh start. From the standpoint of a Buddhist, it means returning to the fundamentals of Buddhism and endeavoring anew for self-improvement.

Upon Rissho Kosei-kai's sixtieth anniversary, then, it was important that we return to the starting point of the organization and, like newborn babies, make a fresh start, engaging anew in endeavor. Most important was that each and every one of us bring the Buddha's teachings alive in our daily lives and till the field of the heart.

In the first sixty years we devoted ourselves to the objective of "dedicating ourselves to the salvation of each and every person," the vow of Rissho Kosei-kai at the time of its founding and the vow of the Buddha. "Tilling the field of the heart" sounds a bit different, but there is no real difference in the underlying vow, since tilling the field of the heart means being saved.

"Each and every one of us tilling the field of the heart" strongly connotes looking within ourselves—and, even more strongly, first undergoing a great transformation. "Dedicating ourselves to the salvation of each and every person" expresses the vow to till the field of the heart through the bodhisattva practice, and "each and every one of us tilling the field of the heart" expresses the vow to devote ourselves to the bodhisattva practice by tilling the field of the heart. While the emphasis differs slightly, fundamentally the two objectives are the same. Both involve benefiting oneself and benefiting others, which are equally necessary.

Tilling the field of the heart is important in every age. It is the basis of the Buddha's teachings. Indeed, I believe it is the basis of all religions. When we turn our eyes to the basis of all religions instead of being preoccupied with a particular religion, an expansive world opens up before us.

Looking within

When we think through the vow of the Buddha and the spirit of Rissho Kosei-kai at the time of its founding, we can glean a variety of meanings from the objective of "each and every one of us tilling the field of the heart." Merely being born physically is not enough to make us human. Only when we awaken to the realm of eternal life and are reborn to the realm of the spirit are we truly human. Rebirth as true human beings—this is the realm to which religion aspires. Tilling the field of the heart is indispensable to this rebirth. In other words, to be born again as a human being, to be reborn as a true human being through transformation, is the vow and the goal of "each and every one of us tilling the field of the heart."

As I have already suggested, "each and every one of us tilling the field of the heart" means looking within before looking at the external world, the conditions around one. This is the important meaning of "tilling the field of the heart." Looking deep within is one of the Buddha's teachings, and is basic to the way in which Buddhism builds peace in society and generates individual peace of mind.

Religion, especially Buddhism, emphasizes looking deep within oneself over looking outward and reforming society. By looking within we become aware of the value of life, and that in turn leads to a great transformation, giving us a sense of the oneness of all living things. Buddhism seeks the fundamental solution to human suffering through each and every person's looking within and undergoing a change of heart. That is why the Buddha considered meditation important. Changing external conditions is one prerequisite for bringing about peace, but it does not lead to a fundamental solution of the problem of suffering. It is by looking within oneself and recognizing the Truth and the Dharma that the problem of suffering and all other problems are solved and peace is attained.

Behind the founder's contributions to world peace through interfaith cooperation and his many initiatives in this area lay the fundamental wish that each and every person establish inner peace. I believe it was because he looked deep within himself that he gained the goodwill of religious leaders around the world and was able to expand Rissho Kosei-kai's scope of activities so greatly. In terms of conventional wisdom, looking within oneself is not particularly empowering, but in actuality it is the most empowering thing one can do and is the way to lead people to peace and true happiness.

Tilling the field of the heart has a great impact on those around one. "Believing oneself, one brings others to believe," it is taught. The all-important first step is to establish one's own faith firmly, take refuge in the Buddha, and recognize the Truth and the Dharma.

If the field of the heart is well tilled, we can enjoy lives that are always replete with joy. Instead of criticizing others, let us first recognize the Truth and the Dharma, look within, and joyfully walk the Way of the Buddha. This is the basis of everything.

The fertile field of the heart

The agricultural philosopher Ninomiya Sontoku (1787–1856) wrote, "If you till the field of the heart, tilling the wilderness is easy." In other words, tilling the wilderness is an arduous task, but if you can till the field of the heart you will have no trouble tilling the wilderness.

Buddhism includes the concept of the field of merits (also called the field of blessings). The field of merits is the field that generates virtues, the greatest field of merits being the Buddha. The Threefold Lotus Sutra likens the Buddha to "the blessing-field for gods and men" and "the great field of blessings for all living beings." An old Japanese maxim runs, "Cultivate virtues in the field of merits."

We too are fields that generate merits. As the Sutra of Innumerable Meanings says, "Pouring abundantly the supreme Mahayana, they [the bodhisattva-mahasattvas] dip all the good roots of living beings in it, scatter the seeds of goodness over the field of merits, and make all put forth the sprout of buddhahood." This passage teaches the order in which the buddhas awaken the aspiration for buddhahood in us. This field of merits is none other than the field of the heart within everyone.

Each of us has a distinctive inner landscape. Of course it also shares features with others' inner landscapes, but since we are all discrete beings, our fields of the heart put forth a wide variety of sprouts: compassion, warmth, flexibility, respect for life, and so on. When a field is tilled, its soil is loosened and it yields a rich harvest. In the same way, as we till the field of the heart our stiff and unyielding self-centeredness is loosened, we are released from suffering, and we are reborn as compassionate people imbued with respect for life. The more we till the field of the heart, the richer the harvest we reap. If we give the field water and light, it will yield an abundant harvest. The key is the way we till it. The field of the heart holds boundless potential; originally it is rich and fertile.

Plowing the soil and sowing the seed

I find the image conveyed by the following story from Shakyamuni's forty-five years of teaching especially moving. It appears in many scriptures, including the Suttanipata, the Samyutta-nikaya, and the Samyukta-agama (Grouped Discourses). The version below represents my amalgamation.

Shakyamuni was staying in a brahman village in the kingdom of Magadha. The brahman Kasibharadvaja, a large landholder, had had his workers yoke oxen to five hundred plows in preparation for plowing and sowing and was distributing food for the morning meal. Shakyamuni went there and stood quietly to one side. Seeing him, Kasibharadvaja said accusingly, "Shramana! We plow the soil, sow seed, and thus obtain our food. Why don't you plow your own field and obtain your own food?"

Shakyamuni replied quietly, "Brahman! I too plow the soil, sow seed, and obtain food." Kasibharadvaja, not understanding what he meant, retorted, "Shramana! We have never seen you plowing. Where is your plow? Where is your ox? Please explain what you mean by plowing in a way that we can understand."

Shakyamuni replied with the following verse: "Faith is the seed, penance is the rain, wisdom is my yoke and plow; modesty is the pole, mind is the yoke tie, mindfulness is my plowshare and goad.

"I am guarded in body and guarded in speech, restrained in my belly in respect to food. I make truth my weeding hook and meekness my unyoking.

"Energy is my beast of burden; bearing me to rest from exertion, it goes without turning back to where, having gone, one does not grieve.

"Thus is this plowing of mine plowed. It has the death-free as its fruit. Having plowed this plowing, one is freed from all misery."

Moved by Shakyamuni's words, Kasibharadvaja offered him rice gruel boiled in milk. But Shakyamuni refused it, saying, "It is not the custom of an enlightened one to receive food in exchange for reciting verses." He ordered the brahman to dispose of it in water where no fish, insects, or other living things dwelt. Kasibharadvaja did so, upon which the rice gruel hissed and gave off steam. Seeing this, he pledged himself to Shakyamuni on the spot and begged to be allowed to become a disciple. Eventually he gained the enlightenment of an arhat.

Thus Shakyamuni taught the importance of tilling the field of the heart. The image of Shakyamuni conveyed here and his dialogue with Kasibharadvaja teach us a great deal. Of course we learn that Shakyamuni taught the importance of constantly tilling the field of the heart, but we also learn what tilling the field of the heart actually means and how to go about it.

Each one of us, from our own standpoint, should think about how best to till our own field of the heart and make this our objective. I myself see the objective of "each and every one tilling the field of the heart" as comprising five elements: mindfulness, thanksgiving, mildness, warmth, and the joy of faith. They all seem different, but fundamentally they are linked and together make up an invaluable mind-set.

Mindfulness

Through mindfulness, the essence of religion, we gaze within ourselves and gaze at the source of life. This provides the occasion for tilling the field of the heart.

Religion lays great value on mindfulness, on looking deep within oneself—so much so that we can even equate the two. Religion is found where there is mindfulness; where there is no mindfulness, there is no religion. Thus, the essence of religion is mindfulness. It follows, of course, that the essence of Buddhism is mindfulness. As we know, Shakyamuni gained enlightenment through deep contemplation, that is, mindfulness.

Self-reflection is the inward examination of one's daily actions, one by one. Mindfulness is scrutiny of not only one's individual actions but one's entire inner landscape, oneself as a whole. It means looking at oneself as a whole human being, not just at this or that aspect of oneself.

As living things, human beings are constantly changing; they are not fixed entities. To look at the totality of this ever-changing self is to look at the very self. It is to view the human condition in its entirety. In other words, it is to gaze at the living, moving source of life, the true form of life.

Shakyamuni said to the brahman Kasibharadvaja, "Mindfulness is my plowshare and goad." "Plowshare" refers to the origin or occasion of something, that which triggers it. Mindfulness, then, provides the occasion for tilling the heart.

Mindfulness is possible any time, any place—in a

crowded train on the way to work, in the quiet moments before sleep. Morning and evening sutra recitation is a good time for mindfulness, and there are many other such times and places. If we aspire to constant mindfulness, we can touch the true form of life, the source of life.

Touching the absolute

Gazing upon one's inner landscape, at one's very self, one arrives at something absolute, what the eminent Buddhist educator Shuichi Maida calls "the impulse of life." Labor and childbirth, he points out, do not arise of a woman's own volition. They are natural workings. And the newborn baby's suckling is not a conscious action; it is an impulse or drive.

Likewise, we grow sleepy naturally; it is not something we do deliberately. Hunger, too, is something that occurs naturally, regardless of our will. What causes these phenomena? The same kind of natural working can be seen in regard to emotions. When we are attracted to the opposite sex, it is not because we deliberately set out to be attracted; it just happens. Attraction comes first; we attach reasons to it later. Again, we do not get angry because we decide we are going to. Anger seizes us unawares. Thus, the varied emotions we feel are not subject to our power. They emerge from somewhere beyond ourselves. They are touched off by contact with an irresistible force.

Thought is supposedly a conscious act, but it too is triggered by an irresistible force. If, when we think of something, we are asked why we did so, all we can say is "I don't know, I just did." We can even say that something impelled us to think as we did, that something must have triggered the thought. It is said that human beings do not think about things that are not necessary to their own lives, which means that we think because it is essential to life.

Although we may believe we are doing all this of our own volition, each and every case depends on the working of an absolute force beyond ourselves. In every aspect of daily life we are in touch with something beyond humanity. Through mindfulness we realize that our daily life, our very existence, is informed by an irresistible force, a force beyond humanity. Human beings, with their finite lives, are in touch with infinite life. Individual selves are in touch with an absolute force that transcends the individual.

It is through mindfulness that we become aware of the absolute force within ourselves. We realize that the source of our actions, emotions, and thoughts lies not within ourselves but in this absolute force. We are powerless to sway it, nor can we create or destroy it at our whim. This, indeed, is the true form of life.

We do not live by our own power

Another aspect of mindfulness is that through it we discover that we are sustained by absolute life, that we are enveloped by absolute life and live in its embrace. The intuitive realization that we are given life alerts us to the importance of respect for life. In the exchange between Shakyamuni and Kasibharadvaja, the brahman started out by saying, in effect, that he lived through his own efforts, but Shakyamuni said that the brahman was *given* life. Shakyamuni's whole life was infused by this spirit.

When we pride ourselves on making a living by

creating something through our own labor, we are prone to accuse others of doing nothing. Shakyamuni demonstrated, however, that we do not live by our own power but are given life. This is a key feature of Buddhism. Society takes the narrow view that our lives and achievements depend on our own efforts. Effort is important to life, but the Buddha's teaching is much wider and deeper. Through it we realize the error of priding ourselves on living by our own power, and it awakens us to the fact that our lives are sustained by many other people and by the Buddha.

Shakyamuni's verse prompted Kasibharadvaja to pledge himself to the Buddha on the spot, and eventually he became an arhat. He was transformed by Shakyamuni's words.

The virtue of humility

When we gaze within, we see that we contain both good and evil. It is important to honestly acknowledge this. We are guilty of robbing other living things of life in order to sustain our own lives. But we are also capable of sustaining the lives of other beings. Moreover, within ourselves we find both self-centered greed and the altruistic impulse to improve society. All this indicates our contradictory nature. When we realize this we feel distress and sorrow, but we also become aware of the mystery of humanity. If we bear all this in mind, we will avoid both self-denigration and arrogance.

When we are in conflict with someone, if we honestly examine ourselves we can never say flatly that we are absolutely right. Recognizing our flaws gives us humility, one of the most important virtues. A humble person always lives in accordance with the Truth and the Dharma. The Lotus Sutra and many other sutras begin with the words "Thus have I heard." Following the Buddha's teachings begins with listening to them with an open mind.

Hearing is said to be the most inner-directed of the senses. Sometimes, when we hear another's views, we refuse to accept those that do not agree with us. But the kind of hearing I am talking about here is very different from merely listening to the opinions of seniors and so on. The true meaning of hearing is to efface oneself and fully take in what one hears even if one cannot agree with it. This kind of hearing means setting aside, if only momentarily, the idea that one is right and looking within oneself in the light of another's teachings.

Speaking to the brahman Kasibharadvaja, the Buddha said, "Modesty is the pole." These days *modesty*, in the sense of shame, seems to be a dying word, but traditionally modesty, or shame, has been a highly valued virtue in Japan. Seen in Buddhist terms, shame is the gateway to repentance. When one gazes at oneself and becomes aware of the Truth and the Dharma, one realizes how insignificant one is in the face of the infinite. This gives rise to shame, and to repentance. Conceit is severed, and one has no choice but to become humble. One sees the arrogance of one's way of living and is ashamed. One is compelled to bow down before the absolute.

The Japanese expression *ome-ome to ikiru* means to live (*ikiru*) in a shameless or brazen manner (*ome ome to*). It implies a sense of shame for being oblivious to that which we should be ashamed of. Reflection on episodes of daily life can trigger a sense of shame, but that is a superficial kind of shame. The essence of shame—that which we should be most ashamed of— is lack of awe and thanksgiving toward the absolute. True awareness of what we should feel ashamed of springs from self-examination.

Constant mindfulness

Through mindfulness we gaze at our own relative self and the absolute force that transcends it. Even if we gaze within and clearly know our inner landscape through mindfulness, however, there is nothing we can do about it. We cannot improve it, however much we may want to. Mindfulness only lets us know ourselves as we are, only shows us the true form of life of finite human beings. We can observe, know, and realize this, but we cannot change it. Nor can we do anything about the working of the absolute force. It is the working of nature, the working of a force transcending humanity.

We do not change through self-examination. We can only look into ourselves. All we can do through mindfulness is gaze deep within and touch the true form of life. Mindfulness makes clear our complexity and mystery, giving rise to contradiction, confusion, and anguish. It reveals the inevitability of contradiction, confusion, and anguish and makes us realize that this is the human condition.

I imagine that some will wonder whether self-examination can serve as a vigorous power for life. But I believe that mindfulness is the most important source of power. Shakyamuni is the greatest exemplar of a person who has come face to face with human contradiction and touched the absolute through mindfulness. It was through mindfulness that he awakened to the Truth and the Dharma. Knowing this is enough to stop us from dismissing mindfulness as having no power and generating no power.

As I have already noted, if we gaze deep within through mindfulness we become aware of our contradictory nature, made up as it is of both good and evil, both self-centered greed and the impulse to altruism, and we feel confused and anguished. This process is important; if we avoid looking frankly at our contradictory nature and shrink from confusion and anguish, we cannot achieve mindfulness. It is when we confront our contradictions, taste the depths of anguish, and then surmount them that we are reborn.

Human beings are interesting. When we experience anguish over our contradictions, we are moved by the complexity of humanity. Being moved in this way is the essence of what makes human beings interesting, and is the springboard for a new phase of life. Surmounting our contradictions makes us aware of the rich potential of humanity, that amalgam of good and evil, self-centeredness and altruism. We realize the boundless potential of humanity, we are infused with the courage to live, and life's boundless potential unfolds before us. This is the power generated by mindfulness.

Mindfulness dissipates anger and confrontation, gives rise to mildness, and leads to harmony. Mindfulness makes us aware of the mystery and value of life and makes us thankful for everything. Mindfulness frees us from ricocheting between joy and sorrow and lets us remain calm and collected at all times.

We can lead lives that are truly worthwhile, laughing and crying with others, feeling compassion for them, and dedicating ourselves to their well-being. Finally, mindfulness leads to firm belief in the Truth and the Dharma. This is how we encounter the Buddha.

None of this can be achieved by our own power. It is a realm that opens up naturally through what we might call the gift of nature or the gift of the Buddha—the working of the great life force.

Counting Our Blessings

Let us live every day with thanksgiving, counting whatever we see and come across as a blessing. We are all blessed with life.

The ability to accept every day as a blessing and live it with thanksgiving is, I believe, the greatest happiness. I would like to see us live with the focus on how we can maintain this frame of mind. Our greatest blessing is having been born into this world, having been given life as human beings. Life consists of both joy and sorrow, both pleasure and pain. It is because we have been given life that we can taste all this. And it is because human life has been bestowed on us that we can encounter the precious teaching of the Buddha. How blessed we are! To live in thanks for this is what gives our lives significance; it is the leitmotif of life as a human being.

True *joie de vivre* and happiness come from thanksgiving for our own lives. Conversely, if we forget to give thanks for life, there can be no *joie de vivre,* no happiness. At bottom, our lives are linked to the lives of all other beings. And while our lives are finite, they are sustained by an infinite life and thus partake of eternal life. What is more, each and every life is unique; each is distinctive and irreplaceable. Let us live in such a way that we never forget to give thanks for this wondrous life, this blessed life, this irreplaceable life.

Everything is a blessing
When we realize what a blessing our lives are and the impulse of thanksgiving arises within us, we become able to accept everything that occurs around us as a blessing. Joy and pleasure, of course, but also pain and sorrow become blessings. Even those who speak to us harshly and those with whom we are in conflict are seen as blessings. All people are perceived as precious.

Everything is a blessing: being able to wake up in the morning as usual, being able to say good morning to our families, seeing our children set off for school, being able to work. The natural phenomena of rain and sunshine are a blessing, as is the sight of flowering plants and of animals romping. Being healthy is a blessing. And if we fall ill, we realize the joy and blessing of health and thus can give thanks for illness, too. We take the occurrences of daily life for granted, but when we think things through, we see that nothing could be more marvelous. What a blessing the commonplace is!

Daily life means, I think, living with thanks for everything, seeing each commonplace element of everyday life as a blessing and a wonder. To nurture this sensibility is to till the field of the heart. I hope, too, that we will firmly realize that gratitude arises from recognition of transience.

Seeing the unseen

Every Japanese person knows the word *arigatai*, rendered here most often as "blessing." *Arigatai* harbors an important meaning. Its literal meaning is "difficult to have or be." Originally, *arigatai* signifies how very difficult it is for each and every thing to be precisely as it is. We need to clarify what is *arigatai*, what is a blessing. I have spoken again and again about the importance of recognizing transience. This means realizing what is a blessing by identifying what causes us to feel thankful.

The Buddha teaches that having received life as human beings, having come into contact with the Buddha Dharma, and all the commonplace things that we take for granted are occasions for thanks. To accept this fully and feel thankful for everything is to till the field of the heart.

We say thank you (*arigato* in Japanese) when someone has been kind to us or shown us goodwill. But being thankful does not apply only to what suits our convenience; it means being able to say thank you for that which is inconvenient or uncomfortable, as well. It also means being thankful for the working of the fountainhead of all life, the absolute force that sustains all living things.

The majestic tree that withstands wind and rain has long, stout roots stretching deep underground. Those roots, invisible to us, support the great tree. The saying "the tip of the iceberg" means that what we see is only a tiny bit of the whole; the bulk of the iceberg is hidden beneath the surface. And frigid though the water is, under the iceberg are hosts of fish and plankton. What this tells us is that valuable things dwell where we cannot perceive them directly. Our being alive here and now is due to the working of a great life force invisible to us, and we are sustained by its power. In short, we live because we are given life. What a blessing this is! Cultivating the discernment to sense the blessed working of the unseen transforms our life.

Thanksgiving, the foundation of life

Whether we are deeply thankful for having received the precious gift of life and having been born as human beings determines whether we know happiness. The verse in the Dhammapada that reads "Difficult it is being born a human. / Difficult it is being alive now for those for whom death is inevitable" teaches that being able to give thanks for one's own life is the greatest happiness of having attained life in this world.

The key to *joie de vivre* is gratitude for having been given life in this world. If we have a strongly developed sense of gratitude, life becomes firm and solid, and we can live lives full of joy, never wavering. Gratitude for having received life as a human being: When we become aware of this, the foundation of humanity, we can give thanks for everything, even hardship, accepting it with thanks as a time of testing and then rising to the challenge. When we become aware of the blessing and wonder of having received life as human beings, a sense of the value of our own lives wells up within us. We are also compelled to feel the same way about all life.

When we become aware of the blessing of our own lives, we find ourselves unable to fight others. Instead we realize that harmony with others is our true desire and the desire of all people. To become aware of, and live with gratitude for, the blessing and wonder of life, and of having been born as a human being, is the foundation of human life. Herein lies an important aspect of the objective of tilling the field of the heart.

In Praise of Mildness

Recognition of the law of transience opens the way to selflessness and reveals the realm of tranquillity.

Japan is said to have spent the last half century in peace. Whether this has been peace in the true sense, however, is questionable. Looking around the world, we can hardly say that it has been peaceful. To find true peace, all people need to create peace within themselves, desiring peace and striving to attain it.

No amount of external power can bring about peace or fundamentally wipe out conflict. True peace is created only when individuals cultivate mildness within themselves. As with the world and society, trouble, strife, and confrontation between individuals can only be fundamentally resolved when they bring mildness to their dealings with each other.

The Seventeen-Article Constitution of the great Japanese statesman Prince Shotoku begins with the famous words "Harmony is to be valued,"which express a basic and universal human desire. The aim of Buddhism too is harmony. That "harmony is to be valued" is the true path for Japan—indeed, for all of humanity—was articulated by Prince Shotoku some fourteen hundred years ago.

People feel most comfortable, relaxed, and serene when they are in harmony. Replacing "harmony" (*wa*) with "mildness" (*yawaragi*) in the passage quoted above, I feel, conveys the spirit of Prince Shotoku's words still more clearly: "Mildness is to be valued." *Yawaragi* connotes freedom, flexibility, gentleness, and tranquillity. It is the state in which self-centeredness has been totally broken down. Recognition of the law of transience opens the way to the realm of tranquillity.

Leave anger to the other

Shakyamuni's teaching is the teaching of peace. In short, Buddhism equals peace. While it is hard to express what this peace means in just a few words, we can say that where there is violence, there is no peace. Violence takes many forms. Raising one's fist against another is, of course, violence; so is coercing or dominating others. Attempting to manipulate and control others to make them conform to one's own selfish thoughts and desires is violence, as well. When others do not do as one wants, one is stirred to anger. This anger is the root cause of violence.

If people could control and cut off anger, then violence—and thus conflict and war—would disappear. If anger were tamed and converted into mildness, the realm of peace would emerge. Conversely, until anger disappears from people's inner life, there can be no peace. We need to look within and reflect on whether we can really control and cut off anger toward one another. Anger has a major bearing on everything from family peace to world peace.

Article 10 of Prince Shotoku's Seventeen-Article Constitution has this to say about anger: "Let us cease from wrath, and refrain from angry looks. Nor let us be resentful when others differ from us. For all men have hearts, and each heart has its own leanings. Their right is our wrong, and our right is their wrong. We are not unquestionably sages, nor are they unquestionably fools. Both of us are simply ordinary men. How can anyone lay down a rule by which to distinguish right from wrong? For we are all, one with another, wise and foolish, like a ring which has no end. Therefore, although others give way to anger, let us on the contrary dread our own faults, and though we alone may be in the right, let us follow the multitude and act like men."

What should we do when someone displays anger toward us? Prince Shotoku says, "Although others give way to anger, let us on the contrary dread our own faults." In other words, let us ask ourselves what within ourselves has provoked the other person's anger. If we face someone who is angry with us and acknowledge our own faults, the other's anger will fade away.

In most cases, we blame the other person for not understanding our feelings or not knowing the facts. And we react to anger with anger. But as Prince Shotoku says, "Both of us are simply ordinary men." Neither of us is perfect. The other person may be wrong in some ways, but so are we. Can we honestly say that we have done nothing to make the other person angry? It is important that we take note of this. It all comes down to whether we look at our own or the other person's faults first. If we reflect on our own errors and apologize for them, the other person's anger will dissipate.

Generally, when we are tussling we do not hit someone who is down. And when we see a helpless opponent we are driven to reflect on our own behavior. Mutual self-reflection generates mildness, and conflict disappears. What is important is that both parties, instead of assuming that they are absolutely right and totally without fault, reflect on the fact that "both of us are simply ordinary men." It is important to realize that we are not perfect but are "ordinary men" in the eyes of God and the Buddha. This realization makes people gentle, brings peace to the world, dispels confrontation, and gives rise to harmony. When we leave anger to the other person, quietly question ourselves about our own flaws, and are mindful, the other person's anger naturally subsides and the realm of mildness and harmony emerges.

A pliant heart and mind
Tilling the field of the heart means developing a pliant mind—what we might call mental freedom. This kind of flexibility allows us to stop being preoccupied with differences between ourselves and others and to understand our interdependence.

Attachment to things is the cause of suffering. When we understand that everything is impermanent and devoid of self, our minds become flexible and we can become free as attachment falls away. This is the state described in the phrase "nirvana is eternally tranquil." Buddhism calls the state in which defilements have disappeared "nirvana." In today's parlance, this is mental freedom. Since the Buddha's wisdom is infinite, we finite beings can never plumb it. All we can do is approach the infinite by knowing our shortcomings and being humble and pliant.

In a verse in one of the sutras Shakyamuni says, in effect, "Gentleness lifts the yoke from the ox." Pliancy leads to gentleness. Lifting the yoke from the tired ox symbolizes releasing the yoke of suffering from human beings. This verse also conveys compassion for the ox. The ox has worked hard all day and must be tired. In the compassion for the ox that leads to removing his yoke we sense the depth of Shakyamuni's thoughtfulness. The phrase "Gentleness lifts the yoke from the ox" conveys empathy with the life of the ox—the life of which we all partake.

Without gentleness we cannot feel compassion for the ox. This warm consideration is important, reminding us that we must not be rigid. We often say, "So-and-so is always smiling; what a gentle person." Surely what makes us say this is not just the fact that he or she wears a gentle expression, but that we sense the person's compassion for others and empathy with diverse forms of life. This is true pliancy, true gentleness.

Enjoyment through patience

Patience helps us make our way through this world we live in. Patience leads to a gentle heart and mind. Patience means striving to bear up under persecution and humiliation, suffering and disappointment, not succumbing to anger but remaining mild and gentle.

It also means striving not to give way to arrogance or euphoria when praised by others or when brimming over with happiness.

When we talk about patience, we conjure up an image of gritting our teeth and grimly enduring, but essentially patience is enjoyable. The religious and moral philosopher Ishida Baigan (1685–1744), the founder of Sekimon Shingaku—a Japanese movement that syncretized the Confucian philosophy of Wang Yang-ming (1472–1529) and native Shinto and Buddhist thought—said that ideally, patience means ceasing to be conscious of "enduring" or "putting up with" things, accepting this rather as an entirely natural part of life. Enduring is not meant to evoke a sense of pathos or tragedy; it is meant to be done with good humor and enjoyment. When we awaken to the Truth and the Dharma, there is no more grimly enduring with gritted teeth.

Chapter 14 of the Lotus Sutra is titled "A Happy Life." "Happy" connotes not just serenity but also the forbearance that accepts all things. Enduring with good humor and enjoyment means perceiving all difficulties as trials sent by the Buddha. It means seeing difficulties as vehicles through which the Buddha is trying to teach us something, and dealing with difficulties in the realization that it is precisely these difficulties that enable us to savor the spice of life.

In "A Happy Life" we read: "If a bodhisattva-mahasattva abides in a state of patience, is gentle and agreeable, is neither hasty nor overbearing, and his mind [is] imperturbed; if, moreover, he has no laws by which to act, but sees all things in their reality, nor proceeds along the undivided way—this is termed a bodhisattva-mahasattva's sphere of action." When we are able to give thanks for hardship, we have overcome it; and when that happens, a gentler, richer humanity is cultivated.

Chapter 10 of the Lotus Sutra, "A Teacher of the Law," says, "The robe of the Tathagata is the gentle and forbearing heart." This "gentle and forbearing heart," I believe, is the mainstay of a Buddhist.

The world never conforms to our wishes. Nevertheless, we struggle to make things go our way, trying to bend others to our will and acquire all that we want. This is the source of the greater part of suffering. If we accept that the world is intrinsically contrary, we will be able to endure inconvenience as something completely natural rather than growing angry.

Caught up in reality, we tend to forget patience. If we can adopt the approach advised by Ishida Baigan, we will no longer need to think in terms of patience, forbearance, and endurance. If we attain that state of mind, this world becomes the Land of Eternally Tranquil Light, a place of true *joie de vivre*.

"Wisdom is my yoke and plow"

The Buddha said, "Wisdom is my yoke and plow." Wisdom is the working of knowledge of the Truth and the Dharma, the opening of the eye of the Buddha-knowledge, the realization of the law of transience. To say "Wisdom is my yoke and plow" is to say "Realization of the law of transience is my yoke and plow." Wisdom means seeing—and accepting—things just as they are ("things in their reality"). When we look with the eye of wisdom, we see that everything around us is in ceaseless flux, and that all things are linked and interdependent. In short, we perceive the working of the laws of transience and the lack of an abiding self. This is "things in their reality."

If we are preoccupied with the phenomena that directly impinge on us, we lose sight of their essential nature. Conversely, if we are preoccupied with seeing the essential nature of things, we tend to belittle phenomena. It is important to strike a balance, neither belittling phenomena nor losing sight of the essence of things.

Seeing only the surface of things, we alternate between emotional highs and lows. "My kids don't listen to a thing I say." "My husband thinks of nothing but having a good time." "She is totally selfish." Such complaints arise because we are preoccupied with the surface of things. What we need to do is guard against self-centeredness, sensing and considering the other person's feelings. Rather than make up our mind after seeing only one side of things, we need to view things in a multifaceted, holistic, fundamental way. Looking at the big picture is the first step toward acquiring wisdom.

If we can see and accept all things just as they are, we realize that we are all given life, and this totally turns our lives around. Instead of constantly complaining, we find ourselves able to give thanks for everything. Seeing things just as they are is extremely difficult. It is important, though, to liberate ourselves from attachment and develop gentle, pliant, mild minds. This leads naturally to wisdom.

True Human Warmth

Transmitting the Dharma to others is the warmest action in which we can engage. Let us become people imbued with thoughtfulness and warmth and savor the joy of benefiting others.

Tilling the field of the heart means fostering warmth, compassion, and thoughtfulness. All of these are what Buddhism calls donation, or giving. Donation connotes compassion and thoughtfulness; thus, giving means taking thought for the happiness of others.

Giving tends to be thought of as a one-way street—"haves" giving to "have-nots"—but nothing could be further from the truth. Essentially, giving means being *privileged* to provide something to another. In Buddhism, human beings are seen as basically living in a relationship of mutual giving—a relationship of give-and-give rather than give-and-take.

The attitude of society in general is that one is better off receiving than giving, so most people try to amass as many possessions and as much money as possible. This is because they are self-centered and always think of their own benefit first. Of course, in a way, this is natural. But the Buddha said, "First and foremost, give. Put the welfare of others before your own."

Buddhism teaches that one's own true benefit lies in putting the benefit of others first. Giving makes not only the recipient but also the giver happy. Many people have proved this through their own practice. For example, say there are two apples, one bigger and one smaller, and you and another person have to choose between them. If you put your own benefit first, you will reach for the bigger apple. The other person, seeing this, will probably feel disgruntled. If that feeling intensifies, it can lead to outright conflict. If, however, you put the other person's benefit first, you can be content with leaving the bigger apple for him or her. The sight of the other person's beaming face will make your apple taste all the more delicious. Even more important, sooner or later the other person will feel the urge to yield to someone else.

Buddhism teaches that your own benefit and that of others are one and the same. Someone else's happiness makes you happy. This is because giving leads to selflessness and thoughtfulness, so that you and the other person are in harmony. We tend to focus solely on our own benefit and our own family's happiness. Wishing for the other's happiness makes for a warm, big-hearted person. And this leads to harmony with others.

Kind words and a smile

What exactly, though, do we give? Giving can be broadly divided into three categories. The first is spiritual giving—transmitting the Buddha's teachings, the Buddha Dharma, which is the most precious gift a person can receive. The second is helping others with one's body—such as giving one's seat to an elderly person or helping someone with a heavy load; it also includes taking part in volunteer activities. The third is giving wealth—providing aid to those who are financially hard up, donating money for the public good, and so on, to relieve people from hardship.

It is through these three ways of giving that we devote ourselves to others and contribute to their happiness. To those who protest that all this is beyond them, the Buddha teaches that there are things they can give even if they have nothing. Let me tell you about two of them. One is to speak kindly; the other is to interact with others with a smile. Even someone with no material wealth whatsoever can give kind words and a smile. To those who say that interacting with others with a smile is too hard, I recommend practicing smiling in front of a mirror. Even a forced smile makes one feel more cheerful. Whether form or feeling comes first does not really matter. Body and mind are inextricably linked. If you train your body, your mind will become trained; if your mind is upset, your body will be, too. So whichever approach you take— form or feeling—both body and mind will follow suit.

If we are always cheerful and smiling, and speak with kindness and thoughtfulness, what a soothing effect it will have on our surroundings. It will also make us happy. The joy that arises from giving is profound. It is a selfless joy that unites us with others. The joy of receiving cannot begin to compare. The reason is that everyone is endowed with the same precious wish as the Buddha—the wish to make people happy. There is no greater happiness for a human being than to give others joy and happiness. Nothing can take the place of the joy that springs from the satisfaction of having been able to help others. Nothing can impart greater happiness or *joie de vivre*.

Donation, or giving, is one of the Six Perfections of Buddhism. Cultivation of the Six Perfections is regarded as the bodhisattva practice. A bodhisattva is one who strives to emulate the Buddha and aspires to be saved, together with everyone else, by working for the happiness of others. The bodhisattva practice is impossible without a warm heart. At the same time, one can become a warm person through the bodhi-sattva practice.

Sharing the joys and sorrows of others as if they were one's own, and being unable to ignore the misfortune of others, impelled by the wish to help them somehow—this is the wish of the bodhisattva. The practice of devoting oneself to the well-being of others and, spurred by this wish, transmitting the Truth and the Dharma is the bodhisattva practice. Those who are self-centered and in thrall to a relativistic view of things do not know and thus cannot savor the joy of giving. Recognition of the law of transience enables one to begin the quest for harmony with others.

Living with compassion
Chapter 16 of the Lotus Sutra, "Revelation of the [Eternal] Life of the Tathagata," ends with these words, spoken by the Buddha:

> How shall I cause all living beings
> To enter the Way supreme
> And speedily accomplish their buddhahood?

We are always enfolded in the Buddha's great compassion. When we become aware of this great compassion, the vow to live with compassion, like the Buddha, wells up within us. Compassion is not sympathy or pity. It refers to the Buddha's vow to lead all people to the Way of the Buddha and cause them to attain the state of the Buddha. Compassion is when that vow of the Buddha becomes our own vow, which we then transmit to others. Herein lies the true meaning of the bodhisattva practice.

It is very difficult to want to live with the compassion of the Buddha, but if by following the Truth and the Dharma we become able to accept everything that happens to us as a sermon of the Buddha guiding us to the highest Way, we can realize that we are indeed living in accordance with the Buddha's vow. When we become aware that we wish not just for our own happiness but also for the happiness of all those around us, and that we willingly devote ourselves to the happiness of others, a new course opens up before us.

In short, compassion means transmitting the Truth and the Dharma to others, one by one. This is true human warmth. It is the Buddha's vow within us. Firmly aware of this, let us walk the Way of the Buddha.

Giving as a way of life

After gaining enlightenment under the Bodhi tree, the Buddha rose and set out on his travels to teach the Truth and the Dharma that he had realized to others. All his subsequent acts, motivated solely by his awareness of the Truth and the Dharma, can be called "acts of truth." Their aim was to bring all people to an awareness of the Truth and the Dharma.

In the teachings of the Buddha are found these words: "The gift of the Dharma surpasses all gifts. The taste of the Dharma surpasses all tastes. The pleasure of the Dharma surpasses all pleasures." Any kind of giving is precious, to be sure, but teaching others the Dharma is the greatest gift of all. The taste of the

Dharma is superior to that of any delicacy. And the pleasure of savoring the Dharma surpasses all worldly pleasures.

Renouncing his life as a prince and leaving behind his wife and child, the Buddha was enlightened to the great Dharma of the cosmos. Thereafter he continually taught this Dharma to liberate people from suffering. He expressed that state of mind in the following verse from chapter 3 of the Lotus Sutra, "A Parable":

> Now this triple world
> All is my domain;
> The living beings in it
> All are my children.

Making the Dharma his daily bread and teaching on his travels his pleasure, the Buddha dedicated his life to giving people the gift of the Dharma. Nikkyo Niwano, the founder of Rissho Kosei-kai, also continually taught the Truth and the Dharma, wishing for the happiness of others as had the Buddha. As a result, many people have followed the Way of the Buddha, have awakened to what truly makes life worth living, and have been saved.

When we think of the Buddha's life, we become aware of the Truth and the Dharma and transmit it to others, walking the Way of the Buddha together. We then realize that this is what has made our birth as human beings in this world truly worthwhile. In the firm awareness that the Buddha's life was dedicated to spreading the teaching, let us devote ourselves together to following the Way of the Buddha.

The Joy of Faith

To yearn to meet the Buddha, sowing the seed of faith in the field of the heart—this is the source of life, the seed of life's greatest happiness.

When we till the field of the heart, what seed do we sow there? The most important thing in human life is to sow the seed of happiness. We can also call it the seed of life. Or we can call it the spiritual seed, the seed of the innermost human wish.

Shakyamuni told the brahman Kasibharadvaja, "I too plow the soil, sow seed, and obtain food." He also said, "Faith is the seed." The seed we should sow in the field of the heart to gain true happiness is the seed of faith in the Buddha Dharma.

In the *Senjisho* (The Selection of the Time) Nichiren wrote, "How fortunate, how joyous, to think that, with this unworthy body, I have received in my heart the seed of buddhahood!" The seed of buddhahood can also be termed the Buddha-knowledge or the buddha-nature. It is, in short, the potential (the seed) to become a buddha. Sowing the seed of buddhahood within oneself means sowing the seed of faith in the Buddha Dharma. The Buddha used the word *seed* as a metaphor for faith. We plow the soil of the field of the heart and sow the seed of faith. That seed is the very source of life.

The Flower Garland Sutra describes the human condition as follows: "Making their karma the field of an ego, using the activities of the mind as seed, beclouding the mind by ignorance, fertilizing it with the rain of impure desires, irrigating it by the willfulness of an ego, they add the conception of evil, and carry this incarnation of delusion about with them." Ignorance, impure desires, ego, and the conception of evil (misconstruing right as wrong, and vice versa) are sources of delusion. Without realizing it, we accumulate these within ourselves. No doubt there are other sources of delusion, too. Suffice it to say that before encountering the Buddha Dharma we are a veritable mass of delusions. For this very reason, it is important that we till the field of the heart, expose delusion to the light of wisdom, and sow the seed of correct faith.

When self-centered people with no faith in the Buddha Dharma gain great ease, it soon turns to suffering; whenever they obtain what they want, they want still more, and as a result they lose a great deal. In responding to Kasibharadvaja's challenge, Shakyamuni ended his verse with these words: "Thus is this plowing of mine plowed. What one reaps from it is freedom from death. Having plowed this plowing, one is freed from all misery." "Freedom from death" means transcendence of birth and death, release from all suffering.

Because people focus their gaze on what is outside themselves, they tend to believe that poverty, illness, strife, and other sufferings will be alleviated if something external changes. In regard to peace, for example, people focus all their attention on resolving the various outward problems that stand in its way. Until we resolve our own internal problems, however, we cannot resolve external problems. Realization of this—that is, a major transformation of all people—is the priority. To achieve this, too, our major task is to sow the seed of faith in the Buddha Dharma in our own field of the heart and nurture it.

Meeting the Buddha

Despite seeking that which makes life truly worthwhile, we feel unsatisfied with our daily lives. This is because we have not yet met the one who has sought that which makes life in this world most worthwhile. The Buddha sought that which makes life in this world most worthwhile. Therefore meeting and emulating the Buddha is the essential condition for tilling the field of the heart and sowing the seed of faith. Of course, we cannot meet the Buddha in the flesh, so we do so through the medium of his teachings. To recognize the Truth and the Dharma to which Shakyamuni was enlightened and live in accordance with them are to meet and emulate the Buddha.

To encounter the Truth and the Dharma is to live earnestly and honestly, and to value our encounters with other people. Doing so deepens our awareness of the Truth and the Dharma. It is in this way that we can meet the Buddha. For example, one spring day the wind scatters the petals of the cherry blossoms that have been in such glorious bloom. Surely we can see and feel the Buddha in this. Sometimes a casual comment by someone we have run into jolts us into taking another look at ourselves. Surely that person is the Buddha, and those words are the teaching of the Buddha.

There are many people who live cheerfully not only in happy times but also in times of discouragement and suffering, seeing these as trials sent by the Buddha for their benefit. These people, I suspect, have met the Buddha and the Buddha Dharma at a crossroads of life and have been reborn.

In chapter 16, "Revelation of the [Eternal] Life of the Tathagata," the Lotus Sutra teaches that the Buddha is "forever here preaching the Law." If we accept that the Buddha is always nearby, preaching the Law, we will meet the Buddha every day. Indeed, we are meeting the Buddha here and now.

No greater joy than faith

To meet the Buddha, encounter the Buddha Dharma, live earnestly and honestly, and value one's encounters—this is true happiness. According to legend, soon after his birth Shakyamuni declared, "I was born so that people the world over may find the path to happiness. I save all in heaven and on earth. I bring ease to all." If we can truly understand these words, we will have been able to meet the Buddha. Let us gratefully receive the Buddha's message that in all of heaven and earth he alone can bring true happiness to all, helping us deepen our faith together and spread that faith far and wide.

Meeting the Buddha can be summed up as recognizing the law of transience. This is the greatest aim of birth into this world. It releases us from all problems and enables us to live freely. To encounter the Buddha, recognize the Truth and the Dharma, awaken to the preciousness of life, share others' sorrow and suffering and make their joys our own, transmit the Truth and the Dharma to others so that they may awaken to the blessing of having been granted life—for a person of faith there can be nothing that makes life more worthwhile.

Talk of the Truth and the Dharma and of the law of transience sounds rather forbidding. But to encounter the Truth and the Dharma is to meet the Buddha and his Law. It is to take refuge in the Buddha and in the Law and to live in earnest, together with others. Herein are found faith and the essence of tilling the field of the heart.